Environmental Law in Argentina

Second Edition

Julio César Villano

This book was originally published as a monograph in the International Encyclopaedia of Laws/Environmental Law

General Editors: Roger Blanpain, Frank Hendrickx
Volume Editor: Kurt Deketelaere

Wolters Kluwer

Published by:
Kluwer Law International
PO Box 316
2400 AH Alphen aan den Rijn
The Netherlands
Website: www.kluwerlaw.com

Sold and distributed in North, Central and South America by:
Aspen Publishers, Inc.
7201 McKinney Circle
Frederick, MD 21704
United States of America
Email: customer.service@aspenpublishers.com

Sold and distributed in all other countries by:
Turpin Distribution Services Ltd.
Stratton Business Park
Pegasus Drive, Biggleswade
Bedfordshire SG18 8TQ
United Kingdom
Email: kluwerlaw@turpin-distribution.com

ISBN 978-90-411-6162-8

This title is available on www.kluwerlawonline.com

The Author

Julio César Villano graduated as a Lawyer in the Law School of the University of Buenos Aires (UBA) in 1986, attending then a series of studies and two post-graduate courses, specifically, in environment.

He has more than twenty-five years of professional experience in corporate consultancy as a legal environmental adviser for private enterprises, NGOs, public and environmentalist agencies. He was a member of the National Scientific and Technical Research Council (CONICET) for more than ten years. He was awarded with a Post-Graduate Research Scholarship from the University of Buenos Aires (UBA) to investigate environmental and international law matters. He held the positions of legal adviser and legal attorney of shipping companies, namely the main Latin American shipping oil company and COCA COLA FEMSA de Argentina among other corporate organizations. He also advices at the department of environmental control at the port of Buenos Aires. He is the founder of the law firm *E*studio *V*illano – www.estudiovillano.com since 1994 and is co-coordinator of the Legal Advisory Committee of the Argentine Port Board, where he has rendered professional advice on environmental, insurance and environmental regulation matters applicable to port activities.

Before graduating as a lawyer, Julio César was assistant professor in the course at the Faculty of Law of the University of Buenos Aires (UBA) in the 'Legal Regime of Natural Resources'. Since 1986, he has worked as a professor in the aforementioned School of Law (in the past he held the position of acting professor at university and in post-graduate courses) and in other subjects. He has been a Law Professor in the Universitary Institute of the Argentine Navy since 2005.

He is fluent in English, French and Italian. Julio César is member of the City of Buenos Aires Public Bar, the Province of Buenos Aires Bar, the Maritime Law Institute of the National Academy of Law of Buenos Aires, the European Society of International Law (ESIL), Member of the British Institute for International and Comparative Law (BIICL), Member of the Asociación Internacional de Derecho Portuario (Spain) and Member of the Legal Writing Institute (Mercer University).

The Author

Table of Contents

List of Abbreviations

ARN	Nuclear Regulatory Agency
CABA	Autonomous City of Buenos Aires
CARU	*Comisión Administradora del Río Uruguay*
CDM	Clean Development Mechanism
CEAMSE	Ecological Coordination Metropolitan Area
CSJN	National Supreme Court of Justice
COFEMA	Federal Environmental Council
CNRT	National Transport Regulation Commission
Doct.	Doctrine
ECL	Environmental Complexity Level
INTA	National Institute of Agricultural Technology
MERCOSUR	Common Southern Market
N.	Number
NAGO	National Attorney General's Office
NC	National Constitution
PA	Protected Areas
PAEM	Prosecution Agency on Environmental Matters
Regs.	Regulations
SAyDS	Secretariat of Environment and Sustainable Development
SRPC	Special Right for Pollution Control

List of Abbreviations

General Introduction

§1. GENERAL INFORMATION

I. Geography and Population

A. Geography

1. The Argentine Republic is a huge country occupying the southeast portion of the South American continent, measuring not less than 5,000 kilometres in length and approximately 1,200 kilometres in breadth, with a total surface of 2,780,400 square kilometres. It is usually geographically – and not politically – divided into six defined economic regions as follows: the plateau of *Patagonia*[1] (located at the south of the country) the *Central* region[2] (at its centre), the region of *Mesopotamia*[3] (at the north-eastern) the *Cuyo* region[4] (at the centre/northwest), the *North-West* region[5] and the *North-East* region of the country.[6]

The bordering countries are Uruguay, Brazil, Paraguay, Bolivia and Chile.

The legal currency is the Argentine Peso.

The country has an, approximately 5,000 kilometre, coastline, half of which runs alongside the Atlantic Ocean and the Paraná River.

2. The main Argentine rivers are navigable ones and are: the Rio de la Plata (the broadest river in the world) that flows into the Atlantic Ocean, the Paraná river (whose main affluent is the Paraguay River and flows into the Río de la Plata delta) and the Riachuelo river (which is unfortunately known as the *'most polluted river'* in the world) the Pilcomayo, the Bermejo, the Paraná, the Paraguay, the Iguazú and the Uruguay rivers.

3. The soil is fertile, except for the south of the country (Patagonia) which is a dessert. The flora presents enormous wooded regions which cover 20% of the

1. Its provinces are: Neuquen, Rio Negro, Chubut, Santa Cruz, Tierra del Fuego and the Malvinas Islands.
2. Its provinces: Buenos Aires, Cordoba, La Pampa and Santa Fe.
3. Being its provinces: Entre Rios, Corrientes and Misiones.
4. Being its provinces: Mendoza, San Juan and San Luis.
5. Being its provinces: Salta, Jujuy, Tucuman, Santiago del Estero, Catamarca and La Rioja.
6. Being its provinces: Formosa and Chaco.

national territory. Its forests are rich in Monkey Puzzles (Misiones), Schinopsis Balansae (Chaco region), Carob Trees and Aspinosperma quebracho-blanco (Santiago del Estero).

4. Argentina holds more than 400 lakes, some of which are shared with Chile. The main lakes are located to the south of the country, in the provinces of Neuquen, Chubut and Santa Cruz. The 'Argentino Lake' is more than 1,400 square kilometres in size.[7]

B. Population

5. The population of Argentina, according to the last census performed in 2010, is 40,117,096, which represents an increase of 10.6% when compared to 2001. The national population density is 14.4 inhabitants per square kilometre. In the city of Buenos Aires, the population density is 14,450 inhabitants per square kilometre.

II. Legal and Political Structure

A. General

6. According to the National Constitution of 1853 – whose last amendment took place in 1994 – Argentina is politically structured as a federal state divided into provinces, each of which has its own provincial chart or provincial constitution and is legally divided into minor units: the local counties. The national capital is the Autonomous City of Buenos Aires (CABA as per its acronym in Spanish) which enjoys a particular legal hybrid status because it is neither a province nor a county, as the National Supreme Court of Justice (CSJN) decided in *re* 'Gauna' (1997).

7. After the 1994 amendment the National Constitution (NC) provides for attributions to other national bodies or entities: the national General Audit (Article 85, NC), the Ombudsman (Article 86, NC) the Public Ministry (Article 120, NC) the Judiciary Council (Article 114, NC) and the *Jury* (Article 115, NC).

B. Decision-Making Power and Competencies

8. The national government is composed of the following branches: (1) the legislative, which is represented by Congress, whose attributes are set forth under Article 75 of the Constitution, and is made up of two Houses: the House of Representatives (or Deputies) and the Senate; (2) the executive, which is headed by the President of the country, whose main powers and attributes are established by

7. Information from this section comes mainly from these publications: National Geographic Institute, National Institute of Statistics and Census www.indec.gov.ar, La República Argentina www.portal-planetasedna.com.ar.

Article 99 of the Constitution; and (3) the judiciary, which is headed by the National Supreme Court of Jusice (CSJN), whose competence is set forth in Articles 116 and 117 of the Constitution and Law 48 of 1863, as amended.

9. Executive power is vested in the President and also exercised by the Chief Cabinet Minister and fourteen ministries, whose competence is ruled by Law 222520 (Law of Ministries) of 1981. The Ministries are composed by Secretaries, Undersecretaries and Directors. There are also other Agencies and Commissions. The national environmental authority is the Environmental and Sustainable Development Secretariat (SAyDS), which depends on the Chief Cabinet Minister according to Decree 1919 of 2006.

10. The Argentine legal hierarchy is as follows: (1) The NC; (2) international conventions of human rights; (3) other international conventions ratified by Congress; (4) laws passed by the national congress that is the national laws mentioned by Article 75 of the NC (which include the civil, the commercial, the penal and the mining codes and the labour and social security laws); (5) laws passed by each provincial legislative body; and (6) provincial decrees (issued by governors).

11. The federal government, the provinces and the local counties ('*municipios*') all have decision-making power. The law-making instrument of all levels of governments is the *law*. The national Congress and the provincial legislatures both approve law-making instruments named 'laws', while the legislative organs of the '*municipios*' approve law-making instruments named 'municipal ordinances'. The national, provincial and municipal executive powers (i.e., the President of the country, the provincial governors and the county majors, respectively) all approve administrative Acts, named 'decrees'.

12. The country is divided into twenty-three provinces and the CABA.

13. Regarding international cooperation, the federal state has the power to conclude treaties with foreign states according to Article 27 of the NC.[8]

14. The provinces are 'autonomous', which means that they are entitled to pass their own laws and to approve their own constitutions (Article 123, NC) through their provincial legislatures, and to elect their own authorities. All provincial laws must be congruent with the national legislation or national statutory law. Regarding environmental law, the provinces are entitled to set forth stricter environmental standards than those established by the federal laws which set forth the so-called minimum environmental standards. The provinces hold all powers not delegated to the federal government by the NC and also those expressly reserved by special agreements at the time of their incorporation. The 1994 reform added Article 124 to the

8. Said Article reads as follows: 'The Federal Government is obliged to foster its peace and trade relations with the foreign powers through treaties that comply with the public law principles established in this constitution.'

NC, which expressly sets forth that all the provinces have the original ownership of the natural resources existing in their territory. It has to be said that in the 1980s, many provincial constitutions were reformed, and in doing so, they established that the ownership of their natural resources belonged to the provinces and also established environmental rules to improve their inhabitants' quality of life.[9]

15. The provinces are entitled to enter into agreements among themselves (Article 125, NC) and also with foreign states (Article 124, NC). Inter-provincial agreements are limited only to the following purposes: administration of justice, economic interest, and public works and utility. To be valid, these provincial agreements should meet the following conditions: (1) they must be sent to the National Congress for notification (not for approval), (2) they must not be incompatible with the country's foreign policy, (3) they must not affect the federal government's powers and attributes; and (4) they must not affect the nation's public credit. Nothing was said in the NC, before the 1994 amendment, about agreements with foreign states, so many authors concluded that they were neither banned nor permitted.

16. The CABA is entitled to approve its own local constitution, its legislative office, its local judiciary and Supreme Court, and their inhabitants are entitled to vote for national deputies and senators.

17. The counties are local autonomous governments whose existence is granted by Article 123 of the NC, insofar as it clearly establishes that each province approves its own constitution according to Article 5 of the NC, which grants county – or municipal- autonomy to all Argentine provinces.

18. The federal state has the power to conclude treaties with foreign states, according to Article 27 of the NC[10] Regarding international cooperation, the federal state has the power to 'adopt or disregard concluding treaties with other nations and international organizations and the concordats with the Holy See. The treaties and concordats have a superior hierarchy among laws' in accordance with Article 75

9. These were the cases, for instance, of the provincial constitutions of Catamarca (reformed in 1988), Jujuy (1986), San Juan (1986), La Rioja (1986) and others, as it is quoted by María Angélica Gelli *National Constitution Commented and Annotated* (Buenos Aires: La Ley, 2011), 1:571, footnote 1425. This approach matches with the one that prevailed in the USA where '[m]ost federal laws employ an approach under which a federal agency establishes minimum national standards that states may implement themselves of leave implementation to federal authorities. The Clean Air Act, the Clean Water Act, the Safe Drinking Water Act, and federal hazardous waste legislation all require the EPA to set minimum national standards, while authorizing delegation of authority to administer these programs to states. In states that fail to receive program delegation, the laws are administered by federal authorities'. Ronald J. Rychlak & David W. Case, *Environmental Law* 28 (Oceana-Oxford U. Press, 2010).
10. Said Article reads as follows: 'The Federal Government is obliged to consolidate its peace and commerce relations with the foreign powers through treaties that comply with the public law principles established in this Constitution.'

paragraph 22 of the NC, provinces can sign certain types of treaties with foreign states.[11]

19. Regarding environmental laws, after the 1994 constitutional reform, the Federal state has the powers to pass norms with the 'minimum environmental standards', which paved the way to a new understanding of federalism. There is no longer an 'opposition' between the provinces and the federal state, but an 'agreement' between both state levels in which, regarding environmental norms, provinces can set more strict or severe criteria than the Nation, but the provincial environmental standards can never be more flexible and loose or lie below the national ones.

20. The field of political consensus for environmental interaction and complementing action between municipalities, provinces, the CABA and the national state of Argentina, is the Federal Board of Environment (COFEMA), created in 1990 and whose Charter was ratified by Appendix I of Law 25675 of the National Environmental Policy passed by Congress in 2002.[12] In accordance with Article 3 of said Appendix I, the COFEMA is an entity of public law composed by the Argentine provinces, the CABA and the federal state. Law 25670 about Polychlorinated biphenyls (PCBs) and Law 25916 on household waste state that COFEMA is entitled to develop the coordination of policies between provincial and federal environmental norms.

21. Referring back to the minimum environmental standards and as a consequence of an important work with practical interpretation purposes regarding the scope of what must be understood by them, the COFEMA passed its Resolution 92

11. Article 125 of the national Constitution sets forth: 'The provinces can sign partial treaties for the administration of justice, of common interests and common utility tasks, known by the Federal Congress; foster industry, migration, railroad construction and navigable channels, provincial property territorial settlements, the introduction and supply of new industries, foreign capital importation and the exploration of rivers, by protecting laws for these purposes and with their own resources.' Concurrently, the bans for the provinces are set by Art. 126 which reads 'Provinces do not exercise the power delegated to the Nation. They can not sign partial treaties of political nature; neither can they enact trade or internal and external navigation laws: nor even set up provincial customs. They can neither mint currency nor establish notes issuance banks without the Federal Congress authorization. They cannot dictate Civil, Commercial, Criminal or Mining Codes after the Congress has passed them; nor even can they enact citizenship or naturalization laws, bankruptcy, and currency or State document forgery. They cannot establish tonnage rights, nor even build up war ships or armies, save the exterior invasion or imminent danger that does not allow delay, providing due notice then to the Federal Government. They can not designate or receive foreign agents' (the latter is generally called 'right of legation' in public international law).
12. Appendix II of Law 25675 of 2002 approves of the Environmental Federal Pact whose prime objective is 'to foster environmental adequate policies in the whole national territory, establishing Framework Agreements among Federal States and between these and the Nation which would speed up and provide more efficiency to the environment preservation having the postulates of 21 Programme approved by CNUMAD '92 as a reference'.

in 2004, whose first Article defines the content that the minimum environmental standards must have according to what is set forth by Article 41 of the NC.[13]

22. Another topic that the 1994 constitutional reform modified in a significant way is the ownership of natural resources which, in accordance with the new Article 124 of the NC, corresponds to the original domain of the provinces or the federal state depending on the territory that they are located in. The said Article has granted the provinces the power to create regions for their economic and social development and the power to sign international agreements compatible with the foreign policy of the nation. According to Iribarren, the new rules of provincial ownership of natural resources make reference to deep-rooted provincial claims over fishing and hydrocarbon unconstitutionality in which there existed a federal government

13. Article 1 of Resolution 92 of 2004 issued by the COFEMA states: Regarding the content that the minimum environmental standards norms should have of Art. 41 of the National Constitution, the Federal Environment Council owns the definitions and content expressed about it in the Report No 03 of 2004 made by the Permanent Advice Committee of Legislative Consultancy that are mentioned below: Content of Minimum Standards: Minimum Standard is understood as the basic threshold of environmental protection that the National should dictate and that are uniformly in force in the national territory as an irrevocable bottom which guarantees every inhabitant with the minimum environmental protection wherever they may be. It includes those environmental protection concepts and aspects and the technical norms that set values assuring quality minimum levels. The control of the natural resources exploitation and use are legislative powers reserved by Provinces and for that reason it is non-delegated by the Nation. Consequently, the purpose of the minimum standards laws must be that of providing the minimum environmental protection of the resource and not its mere management, an exclusive legislative power of the provinces. Characterization of the Norm Containing Minimum Environmental Standards: Delegation of the legislative power regarding environmental matters. Limitations: it is unquestionable that Art. 41 of the NC has an expressed delegation of the environmental protection legislative powers of the Nations to the provinces, imposing the following limitations for such purpose: (a) the content shall be of minimum guarantee; (b) it shall be of environmental protection; and (c) that local jurisdictions are not altered. 2) They are laws enacted by the National Congress. The mandate of Art. 41 of the NC is granted to the 'Nation' and consists of the passing of 'norms'. In accordance to the provisions in Arts 75, subs. 32, 76 and 99, 2nd paragraph of subs. 3 of the NC, it should be clear that the reference to the Nation is to the National Congress, sole body with legislative powers. Consequently, the concept of 'norms' corresponds to that of laws, which due to its nature, are passed by the National Congress, -Environmental Protection Content: Every interpretation must have a restrictive nature, which implies that its objective must have a direct and concrete relation with the environmental protection purpose without distorting the competencies reserved for the provinces, emptying Arts 122 and 124 out of N.C. – Complementary norms: the minimum standards laws may be ruled by provinces in accordance with the mechanisms foreseen in their normative regulations, in case these consider it necessary for its effective enforcement. However, the Nation has the same power in its jurisdiction framework and in the constitutionally delegated competencies field. From the very own legal nature of the executive regulations, there derives the function of granting operational capacity to those parts that due to its nature do not have them, lacking sufficient entity so as to introduce alterations to them, since regulations cannot go beyond what was anticipated by the legislator. It must be understood that if there exist less restrictive provincial or local norms than the minimum standards law, they must adapt to the National Law. Regarding local norms in force existing before the environmental protection minimum standards laws, they would remain in force provided they are not opposite and are more demanding than these ones.

excess to the detriment of the non-delegated powers, by the provinces, according to some different specialists' opinions.[14]

III. Economic Characteristics

23. The Gross Domestic Product (GDP) was Argentine Peso (ARS) 380 billion in 2010. The annual real growth rate was 7.5% in 2010 (est.). The GDP per capita was ARS 9,400 in 2010. The natural resources are fertile plains, zinc, copper, manganese, iron, oil and uranium.

24. Agriculture represents 8.5% of the GDP. Industry represents 31.6% of the GDP and mainly consists of oil refining, food processing, machinery and equipment, textiles, chemicals and petrochemicals.

25. Its trade comprises oilseed by-products, vegetable oils, cars, grains, its major markets being Brazil, EU, China and USA.

IV. Social and Cultural Characteristics

26. The ethnic groups are: European (97%, mostly of Spanish and Italian descent), mestizo and Amerindian (3%).

27. The language is Spanish and education is compulsory until age 18. The country has a literacy rate of 98%. The infant mortality rate is 10.81/1000 and the average life expectancy is 76 years.

V. Main Environmental Problems

28. Long ago, it was pointed out by many authors that the problems of air, water and soil pollution are centred mainly around a fluvial axis along the borders of the La Plata and Paraná rivers, from the city of La Plata up to the city of Rosario. The mentioned region comprised the western zone of the province of Chaco and the province of Formosa, where 'factors of ecologic disturbance' exist, and have caused the soil to become a desert region.

According to the World Wildlife Fund 'deforestation and pollution are the main threats to Argentina's biodiversity and landscapes'. Beef production also poses a danger to the country's natural habitats. The mentioned foundation explains that:

---

14. Federico Iribarren, *Acerca del Dominio Originario de los Recursos Naturales*, Work published on the Secretariat of Environment and Sustainable Development website, S/D. www.ambiente.gov.ar/archivos/web/PCCGDBM/File/APMC/Jurisprudencia/recursos%20naturales.pdf (accessed 14 Apr. 2011).

> [r]esearch in Argentina has shown that deforestation due to agricultural expansion of soybean is threatening the Yungas 'cloud forest', and the Chaco ecoregion, one of the largest forested biomes (a major regional group of distinctive plant and animal communities) in South America. In Argentina, while most recent expansion in soybean agriculture has relied on available agricultural land, there are aggressive targets to expand the agricultural area to increase soybean production for export.[15]

29. Furthermore, it hast to be noted that the country lacks Environmental Compliance and Enforcement (ECE) indicators. As was recently studied, the primary concerns about them are that the different challenges that must be improved in order to analyse and design ECE indicators in the country are: a new legal environmental framework, different levels of government with environmental responsibilities, environmental strategic plans, prioritization of environmental concerns in the public budget, more developments in the right to access to environmental public information and a more complete and accurate environmental information public system.[16]

§2. Basic Principles of Environmental Law

30. The Argentine legal doctrine has a large background, in terms of the origin, sense, nature, individualization and scope of the different environmental law principles of the country. Although we cannot delve into details, we must point out that his analysis is extremely interesting, especially to show how the Argentine thoughts have evolved since Professor Guillermo J. Cano, a pioneer in the country's environmental law, announced and analysed them with outstanding lucidity in the 1970s, when the University of Buenos Aires Faculty of Law conducted no courses named 'environmental law'. Instead of that, the courses were referred to as 'Natural Resources Legal Regimes' (in which the author of this monograph had the good fortune to participate as Assistant Professor).

31. Article 4 of Law 25675 of 2002 on Minimum Standards on Environmental Protection sets forth ten principles to which 'the construction and application of this law and any other rule on environmental policy' is subject. These principles are the congruency, prevention, precaution, intergenerational equity, progressivity,

---

15. The report is based on studies by A. Dufey, D. Baldock & M. Farmer, *Impacts of Changes in Key EU Policies on Trade and Production Displacement of Sugar and Soy* (2006). Study commissioned by World Wildlife Fund (WWF) to International Institute for Environment and Development (IIED), with the collaboration of Intelligent Energy Europe (IEE) 180 and C. Carey & D. Oettli, *Determining Links between Agricultural Crop Expansion and Deforestation*. A report prepared for the WWF Forest Conversion Initiative (2006), 71. See http://wwf.panda.org/who_we_are/wwf_offices/argentina/environmental_problems_argentina/ (accessed 16 Sep. 2011).
16. María Eugenia Di Paola, *Environmental Compliance and Enforcement indicators in Argentina: Primary Concerns*. Fundación Ambiente y Recursos Naturales (FARN). On the internet it is available at: www.inece.org/indicators/proceedings/04a_argentina.pdf (accessed 26 May 2010).

accountability, subsidiarity, sustainability, solidarity and cooperative principles. We will analyse them below in terms of their practical importance and case law basis.

32. The congruency principle requires that every provincial and municipal environmental law adapt itself to the provisions and principles of Law 25675 of 2002. If that is not the case, the latter shall prevail. It is primarily focused on providing consistency to the Argentine legal system, by determining the national legislation prevalence in case of inadequacy of less hierarchical provisions. It was well recalled that this principle is very similar to the *comprehensive legal regulation principle* and 'it is applicable to almost all international legal instruments and has been recognized at the First Programme of Community Action in the field of Environment, as well as being included under Recommendation 70 of the Action Plan at the Stockholm Conference'.[17]

33. The prevention principle calls for an urgent comprehensive address of the grounds and sources for environmental problems to prevent the negative effects that they may have on the environment. There is no doubt that this is one of the most important environmental law principles, and Argentine case law has always considered it so. 'Environmental prevention is of paramount importance vis-à-vis other fields because environmental damage is expressed in events that cause actual depletion.'[18]

34. The precautionary principle sets forth that, in case of severe or irreversible damage, the lack of information or scientific certainty shall not be used as ground to delay the adoption of efficient measures based on costs to avoid environmental degradation. As it can be seen, not every risky situation deserves the application of this principle. The situation must either be serious or irreversible.[19] This principle's advantages are not unanimously accepted by doctrine.[20]

---

17. Néstor A. Cafferatta (dir), *Summa Ambiental* (Buenos Aires: Abeledo Perrot, 2011), 1:343.
18. Case *Almada, Hugo v. Copetro SA y otros*. Supreme Court of the province of Buenos Aires. Ruling dated 19 May 1998 as published by La Ley 1999, vol C, 1129.
19. To better analyse the scope assigned by case law to this principle in the light of hazardous waste generated at feedlots, it is worth considering the research work carried out by Dr Alba del Valle Thomas Hatti named *Principio Precautorio en Materia Ambiental: Su Aplicación a los residuos peligrosos que generan los feed lots. Concepto, Fuente Normativa y Aplicación Jurisprudencial en la Provincia de Buenos Aires*. This study has been prepared for the National Office of Agriculture and Livestock Trade Control (Oficina Nacional de Control Comercial Agropecuario (ONCCA)) in July, 2010. The author clearly explains in her study, that 'This principle (included in Article 4 of the General Environment Law 25675) differs from the prevention principle (also set forth in Article 4 of Law 25675) in that the precautionary principle involves a more advanced theory and operates when there is uncertainty, while the prevention principle operates on certainty. Furthermore, an efficient application of the precautionary principle demands "the clarification of a potential damage and the existence of scientific principles", according to the conclusions drawn on the General Environment Act and the Precautionary Principle set forth by the National Secretary of Environment and Sustainable Development Workshop organized on 06.26.03.'
20. For example Cass R. Sunstein in his paper *Beyond the Precautionary Principle*, published by The Law School, The University of Chicago, January 2003, considers that 'The precautionary principle has been highly influential in legal systems all over the world. In its strongest and most distinctive forms, the principle imposes a burden of proof on those who create potential risks, and it requires

35. The intergenerational equity principle demands the appropriate use of the environment by current generations, insofar as it is consistent with future generations' rights.

36. According to the principle of progressivity, the environmental goals should be gradually achieved through interim and final objectives, as forecasted in a temporary schedule.

According to the principle of accountability, the person causing a current or future damage to the environment shall bear the costs of every preventive and corrective action, regardless of the environmental accountability systems applicable. As the legal doctrine explains, 'any person generating an environmental "risk" shall repair the damage regardless of the concurring and supplementary application of "solidarity" as another objective attribution factor'.[21]

37. According to the principle of subsidiarity, the national government shall cooperate and offer supplementary participation in environmental protection against acts carried out by individual parties.

38. The sustainability principle requires appropriate environmental management for the economic and social development and the use of natural resources so as not to affect opportunities. This principle is directly related to Article 41 of the NC and the *Our Common Future* Report (Bruntland Report) adopted by the United Nations in 1998, among others.

39. The solidarity principle makes national and provincial governments accountable for the prevention and mitigation of cross-border adverse environmental effects

---

regulation of activities even if it cannot be shown that those activities are likely to produce significant harms. Taken in this strong form, the precautionary principle should be rejected, not because it leads in bad directions, but because it leads in no directions at all. The principle is literally paralyzing-forbidding inaction, stringent regulation, and everything in between. The reason is that in the relevant cases, every step, including inaction, creates a risk to health, the environment, or both'. See http://ssrn.com/abstract_id=307098 (accessed 15 Nov. 2010). Accordingly, Dr Phillipe Malaurie, Emeritus Professor at the University Panthéon-Assas (Paris II) has recently wrote in his book *Droit Civil Illustré* (France, Defrénois Lextenso Éditions, Juillet 2011), 21 that the precautionary principle has 'perverse effects' pointing out 'Ce principe est, depuis 2004, une règle supra-juridique dominant toutes les autres car il a été consacré par L'Art. 5 de la Charte de l'environnement, devenu un principe constitutionnel (préambule de la Constitution, al.1) Comme toutes les règles de droit (et toutes les autres activités humaines), il a des effets pervers, particulièrement nocifs, car son imprécision en fait une source possible d'immobilisme paralysant l'action: il redoute les risques sans exceptions, même purement hypothétiques et pour y échapper impose de ne rien innover'. Regarding the influence of mentioned principle in the European Union law, Elizabeth Fisher explains that the precautionary principle 'has seemingly become a "touchstone" for thinking about the challenges involved in regulating risk in a globalizing world, concerning as it does both the internal and external exercise of state power (de Sadeleer 2002, Wiener and Rogers 2002). As this is the case the principle is an excellent, albeit daunting, starting point for thinking about, and comparing national, EU, and international regulatory models for risk standard setting'. Elizabeth Fisher, *Opening Pandora's Box: Contextualising the Precautionary Principle in the European Union*. University of Oxford Faculty of Law Legal Studies Research Paper Series, Working Paper N° 2/2007, January 2007. On the web: http://papers.ssrn.com/ Abstract=956952 (accessed 18 Dec. 2010).

21. Cafferatta, *supra*, v. 1, 345.

resulting from their own actions, and also makes them accountable for the reduction of environmental risks on shared ecological systems.

40. The principle of cooperation requires the rational and equitable use of natural resources and shared ecological systems, as well as joint actions to reduce cross-border environmental emergencies.

§3. Historical Background

41. Europeans arrived in the region with the 1502 voyage of Americo Vespuccio. The brave Spanish navigator Juan Diaz de Solis visited what is now Argentina in 1516. Spain established a permanent colony on the site of Buenos Aires in 1580, although initial settlement was primarily overland from Peru. The Spanish further integrated Argentina into their empire by establishing the Vice Royalty of Rio de la Plata in 1776, and Buenos Aires became a flourishing port.

42. Argentina formally declared independence from Spain on 9 July 1816. Following the defeat of the Spanish, centralist and federalist groups waged a lengthy conflict between themselves to determine the future of the nation. A modern constitution was promulgated in 1853, and a national unity government was established in 1861. Two forces combined to create the modern Argentine nation in the late nineteenth century: the introduction of modern agricultural techniques and integration of Argentina into the world economy. Foreign investment and immigration from Europe aided this economic revolution. Investment, primarily from Britain, came in such fields as railroads and ports. As in the United States during this same period, the migrants who worked to develop Argentina's resources – especially the western Pampas – came principally from throughout Europe.

43. From 1880 to 1930, Argentina became one of the world's ten wealthiest nations as a result of the rapid expansion of agriculture and foreign investment in infrastructure. The Great Depression brought a halt to this period of booming expansion, and combined with other social and political changes to usher in a period of less stable governance. The governments of the 1930s attempted to contain the currents of economic and political change that eventually led to a military coup and the subsequent emergence of Juan Domingo Peron. New social and political forces were seeking political power, including modern military and labour movements that emerged from the growing urban working class.

44. The military ruled in Argentina's at the beginning of the 1940s. In the 1950s and 1960s, military and civilian administrations alternated the government of the country trying to deal with diminished economic growth and continued social and labour demands. Military and constitutional governments came one after the other until in 1983 democracy returned to the country and is lively since then.

45. Regarding the government and democracy's environmental efficacy issue, it is interesting to highlight the viewpoint that considers the environmental law as a human right from an approach analysed by Zonis[22] in Argentina (among other authors, as we will see in paragraph 97), and by Damilola S. Olawuyi abroad as we will see in paragraph 96 of this work.[23]

§4. The Role of Governmental Institutions in the Shaping and Administration of Environmental Law and Policy

I. General Rules

46. According to Article 41[24] of the NC, the minimum environmental standards are set forth by the federal government for the whole country, and the provinces are enabled to implement those minimum environmental standard rules 'to complement' the national environmental laws. Provincial environmental standards may be higher or stricter than the federal ones, but they must never be more flexible or situated 'below' the national environmental standards.

47. In enacting those legal rules, the national Congress has passed the following eight minimum environmental standards' laws: (1) Law 25612 of 2002 on Minimum Environmental Standards for the Management of Industrial Waste and Service Activities Waste; (2) Law 25670 of 2002 on Minimum Environmental Standards for the Management and Elimination of PCBs; (3) Law 25675 of 2002 on Minimum Standards for the Sustainable and Proper Management of the Environment; (4) Law 25688 of 2003 on Environmental Management of Water; (5) Law 25831 of 2004 on Access to Environmental Public Information; (6) Law 25916 of 2004 on Management of Domestic Waste; and (7) Law 26331 of 2007 on Minimum Standards for

22. Federico Zonis, *La Calidad de las Democracias y la Eficacia del Derecho Ambiental* (SL, SD). This author concludes that human rights are 'all-encompassing of civil, political and social rights. Environmental law is a human right, essential in the citizen as freedom and equality are. By analysing the quality of democracy – that is, the effective enjoyment of fundamental rights by citizens, the institutions' development level and the forms of indirect or direct participation- we can measure the environmental efficacy of a society. I finish saying then that environmental efficacy, as the real and effective right to enjoy a healthy and balanced environment, has a directly proportional relation with a state's democracy quality level.'

23. Damilola S. Olawuyi, *Adopting the Language of Rights for Environmental Protection: Legal and Theoretical Justifications* (United Kingdom: Oxford Student Legal Studies Paper No. 11/ 2011, 21 Oct. 2011). The author of mentioned article explores the debates of whether to treat environmental violations as human rights violations. Full text of this excellent paper is available at the website of the Social Science Research Network http://ssrn.com/abstract=1947545 (accessed 24 Oct. 2011).

24. This Article reads: 'Article 41. All inhabitants are entitled to a healthy and balanced environment fit for human development, so that productive activities satisfy current needs without compromising those of future generations, and have the duty to preserve the environment. Environmental damage shall generate as a priority the obligation to repair it under the terms that the law shall establish. The authorities shall provide for the protection of this right, for the rational use of natural resources, for the preservation of the natural and cultural patrimony and of biological diversity, and for environmental information and education. It falls to the national jurisdiction to dictate laws containing minimum standards necessary for protecting the environment, and to the provinces to dictate those laws necessary to complement the national laws, without such laws altering local jurisdictional authority. The entry into the National territory of dangerous or potentially dangerous wastes and of radioactive materials is prohibited.'

the Environmental Protection of Native Forests; and (8) Law 26562 of 2009 on Environmental Protection for the Control of Burn-Out Activities in the country.

48. All these national laws are complemented by a great number of statutory rules. Many of them were reglamented by the national Executive Power (the President of the country) by issuing the so-called Decrees of the national Executive Power.

49. Other complementary rules, with lower juridical hierarchy than the Decrees of the Executive Power, were passed by the national Secretariat for the Environment and Sustainable Development (SAyDS), which is the national environmental Authority and issues administrative acts named 'Resolutions'.

II. Regime of Access to Environmental Public Information

50. In 2003, Argentina adopted Law 25831 which has not been reglamented yet, and establishes 'the minimum requirements of environmental protection to guarantee the right to access the environmental information in the hands of the state, in national, provincial and municipal field and in the city of Buenos Aires, as well as in autarkic entities and lending companies of public services, either public, private or mixed'.[25] As it can be seen, this norm obliges only the state and the private companies which supply public services. Many big Argentine corporations, however, regularly prepare their public Sustainability Reports, as we will see in paragraph 104 of this work.

As regards the right of information, the National Executive Order 1172/2003 has been in force since 2003 in Argentina. Although it is *widely and generally* applied in the public administration, it requires that the Executive Branch (i.e., the President, Ministries, Secretaries and agencies) and public utility services provide all the information produced by the State, except for data that such National Executive Order and any other law do not allow (such as the State's strategy in a proceeding, bank accounts' data, national security data, trade secrets, political preferences and the sexual orientation of people). Such information must be submitted in writing and free of charge within ten business days with the copies that may be requested. The absence of response will give rise to an appeal. Among the information that can be requested by any individual or artificial person without the need of providing the grounds thereof and of setting up domicile in the city of Buenos Aires we can mention written documents, recordings, pictures and documentation in magnetic, digital or other medium.

As we have already mentioned, this executive order is of general application and does not specifically refer to environmental issues. This does not mean that environmental issues do not fall within its scope. In fact, it has been used several times in practice before Law 25831 was passed.

25. Article 1 of law 25831 of 2003.

51. This regime guarantees the 'free of access for any legal person or individual, except for those expenses related to the used resources for the delivery of the requested information' adding that 'in order to have access to the environmental information it is neither necessary to give reasons nor have determined interest'. It will be enough to present a written request identifying the applicant of the information requested. Said application must be answered in a maximum term of thirty days.

52. The COFEMA is entrusted with the task of establishing the criteria to set the procedures for the access to the environmental information in every jurisdiction (national, provincial, municipal and in the city of Buenos Aires). The information can be refused[26] only when: (a) the national defence, the homeland security or the international relations are affected, (b) the requested information is subjected to consideration of judicial authorities or its dissemination or use by third-parties may cause damage to the normal legal procedure development, (c) the commercial or industrial secret or property rights are affected, (d) the personal data confidentiality is affected; (e) the requested information belongs to scientific researches and they have not been published yet, (f) when the reason for request cannot be determined because of lack of sufficient data or inaccuracy; and (g) when the requested information is classified as secret or confidential by the law.

53. Public servants/officials who fail to comply are exposed to sanctions established by Law 25164 of 1999, which rules the national public employment. If the one who fails to comply with this obligations is a public service company, then the 'corresponding sanctions' are contemplated according to the concession contract, without prejudice of the civil and criminal responsibilities that may correspond.

§5. Sources of Environmental Law

54. As Shelton and Kiss explained:

> [e]nvironmental law, being a relatively new field, is largely contained in written texts, although some common law principles are relevant and customary international law is emerging. Governments protect the environment on the basis of their various constitutional and statutory powers to promote the general welfare, regulate commerce and manage public lands, air and water. National authorities may accept additional duties to protect the environment by entering into bilateral and multilateral treaties containing specific obligations. Promulgation of regulations and permits by administrative authorities is another important source of environmental law.[27]

26. Article 7 of this law.
27. Dinah Shelton & Alexandre Kiss, *Judicial Handbook on Environmental Law* 7 (UK: United Nations Environmental Programme 2005).

55. We consider that the sources of the environmental law can be classified into the international or external sources, which are those norms that the national state receives or boosts to build in the international community acting together with other states by concluding bilateral negotiations or through the conduct of international organizations, and the national sources or internal ones. These are passed by the competent national body -the national Congress in Argentina- acting in its legislative capacity for the whole country. The external sources will be analysed further in section I of this §5, under the heading: 'External Norms'. Below, we will discuss the internal sources in the three Argentine state levels: national, provincial and municipal.

56. In the Argentine law system internal sources of law are split among the following structures: (1) the NC, (2) The International Conventions on Human Rights which were given a constitutional status by the 1994 amendment, (3) international law rules, (4) national statutory law; (5) provincial statutory law, (6) county's statutory law and, (7) city of Buenos Aires statutory law.

57. Specifically, the main source for the national environmental law is the NC, which sets the normative bases in all the Argentine territories, grants functions to the three branches of government and distributes the competencies between the national and local states.[28] With the 1994 reform of the NC, the right of all inhabitants to have a healthy, balanced and proper environment for human development, was included. It also boosted the right to preserve the environment. Besides, it also incorporated the principle of the sustainable development and the obligation of counterbalancing the environmental damage. In essence, it is an obligation for the state to provide the environment right protection, the rational usage of the natural resources, the natural and cultural heritage preservation, the biologic biodiversity preservation, the environmental information and the environmental education. Moreover, it classifies the entry of dangerous or potentially dangerous to the country as a constitutional prohibition, since it was included in the Article 3 of Law 24051 of hazardous wastes of 1992.

58. The provinces are independent and they keep all the power that has not been expressly delegated by the NC to the federal state. These provinces and the city of Buenos Aires are ruled by their own regulations, which are passed by their respective executive branches.

59. The municipalities (also referred to as 'counties') pass regulations and rules to apply within their respective territorial jurisdictions and in the areas of local competence such as the hygiene and the public utility services.

28. Article 75, paras 12, 13, 18, 19, 24, 30 and 32, and Arts 31, 121, 125 and 126 of the national Constitution.

I. External Norms

60. In America, a unique common political and legal system has not been reached so far, like in the European Union, as with Community Law;[29] thus, it is not advisable to make reference to supranational norms, given the non-existence of a supranational body or agency with legislative powers to be imposed on the states of the American region.

61. The external sources of the Argentine environmental law are fundamentally represented by agreements in the sphere of the United Nations and by regional agreements especially in the management of shared basins.

62. Argentine is part of the Common Market of the South (MERCOSUR are per its acronym in Spanish) together with Uruguay, Brazil and Paraguay.[30] Following the principles of the Rio Declaration on Environment and Development of 1992, the Member States of the MERCOSUR signed the Framework Agreement on Environment of the MERCOSUR. Argentina adopted it through Law 25841 of 2004. Said framework agreement obliges states to increase the information exchange on legal norms, to promote policies and national instruments to optimize the environment management, to harmonize their environmental legislations, to promote economic instrument of sustainable development support and timely inform the environmental disasters and emergencies that could affect other states. In addition, Argentina has signed bilateral environmental agreements for water flows with Uruguay, Brazil, Paraguay and Bolivia.

63. Analysing the international environmental law in Argentina implies making a compulsory reference to the milestone writings of eminent national scholars Dr Zeballos de Sisto and Dr Drnas de Clément, at least.

64. Dr Zeballos de Sisto already in 1996 systematized its evolution in an important work explaining that 'the environmental consciousness in the relationship between states started growing by the end of 1800'.[31] This distinguished Argentine

29. The *Enciclopedia Jurídica* Wolters Kluwer (Spain) defines the concept of 'Community Law' as 'the normative system created by the Member States of the European Communities or the European Union (the Lisbon Treaty of 2007 legally established the single denomination of European Union) or by their institutions with legal efficacy for both those and these. It is about an enormous normative material elaborated beyond our border by supranational institutions that, since the beginning of its approval and publishing in the community area, spreads all its efficacy in our territory [making reference to Spain] – the rights acknowledgement and the duties imposition included – prioritizing any other internal norm'. Enrique Arnaldo Alcubilla, *Enciclopedia Jurídica* (Madrid: La Ley Grupo Wolters Kluwer España, 2008–2009), 8:4167.
30. MERCOSUR was created by the Asunción Treaty, Paraguay 1991 with the objective of fostering free flow of goods, services and production factors and to establish an external tariff and a common trade policy. Its Permanent Administrative Secretariat is based in Montevideo (Uruguay). Venezuela is getting incorporated. Bolivia, Chile, Colombia, Peru and Ecuador are associate states. Mexico is an observer in the MERCOSUR.
31. María Cristina Zeballos de Sisto, *El Derecho Ambiental Internacional: Esquema de su Evolución* (Buenos Aires: SE, 14.10.96), 1. In this work, the author highlights 'the formulated complaint in

jurist analyses the different stages in the evolution of the international environmental norms since the time of the hats 'with multiple feathers that Queen Victoria promoted' (which was considered as an example of her origins) mentioning the first international instruments up until the end of the World War I, since 1945 up until the United Nations Conference on the Human Environment (Stockholm 1972), the agreements and treaties signed as of 1972 and the Conference on Environment and Development (1992) in Rio de Janeiro.

65. However, the emeritus professor of the Catholic University of Córdoba, Dr Drnas de Clément analysed 'the importance of the study of the formal sources of the International Law on Environment (DIMA as per its acronym in Spanish), providing these "sources" make-up the legal subsystem of that field of the Public International Law, as a group of norms and principles from which rights and obligations regarding international subjects environment emerge'[32]

66. From the point of view of the international treaties approved, we will say that many environmental agreements were passed by Argentine national laws. Among them, mention has to be made of the following ones:[33]

– Environment Treaty of the Republic of Bolivia: Law 24774.
– Convention for the preservation and management of the Vicuña: Law 23582.
– Convention on the World, Cultural and Natural Heritage Protection: Law 21836.
– Protocol of Montreal regarding Substances that Deplete the Ozone Layer: Law 25389.
– 169th Treaty of the International Labour Organization on Indigenous People and Tribes in Independent Countries: Law 24071.
– Framework Agreement on MERCOSUR Environment: Law 25841.
– United Nations Conference against Desertification and Drought: Law 24701.
– Basel Convention on the Control of Transboundary Movements of Hazardous Wastes and their Disposal: Law 23922.
– Stockholm Convention on Persistent Organic Pollutants (POPs): Law 26011.
– Rotterdam Convention on the Prior Informed Consent Procedure for Certain Hazardous chemicals and Pesticides in International trade: Law 25278.
– Kyoto Protocol: Law 25438.
– Joint Convention on the Safety of Spent Fuel Management and on the Safety of Radioactive Waste Management: Law 25279.

1868 to the Ministry of Foreign Affairs of the Austro-Hungarian Empire by a group of farmers concerned by depredation of insectivorous birds carried out by the feather industry very much developed due to a Victorian fashion which imposed feather everywhere. They asked Emperor Franz Joseph I the subscription to an international treaty to protect those beneficial birds for farming'. Published in www.gnc.org.ar (accessed 15 May 2011).

32. See Zlata Drnas de Clément, 'Fuentes del Derecho Internacional del Medioambiente', in *Environmental Law*, ed. F. Sindico (London: CMP Publishers, University of Surrey, 2010), 1. Available on Academia Nacional de Derecho y Ciencias Sociales de Córdoba website at: www.derecho.unc.edu.ar/ archivo/intpublico/fuentes-der-ambiental.pdf (accessed 18 Sep. 2011).

33. Source: Secretariat of Environment and Sustainable Development (SAyDS) website: www.ambiente.gov.ar (accessed 11 Nov. 2011).

- Convention on International Trade in Endangered species of Wild Fauna and Flora (CITES): Law 25337.
- Annex V to the Protocol of the Antarctic Treaty: Law 25260.
- Additional Protocol on the Conservation and Development of the Fish Resources in the Parana and Paraguay Rivers between Argentina and Paraguay: Law 25048.
- Convention on the Preservation of the Fish Resources of the Paraná and Paraguay Rivers between Argentina and Paraguay: Law 25105.
- Comprehensive Nuclear Test Ban Treaty: Law 25022.
- Convention on Cooperation on Environment signed with Brazil: Law 24930.
- Convention on Prevention and Control of Professional Risks by Carcinogens: Law 21663.
- Convention on Cross-border Health and its Additional Protocol signed with the Republic of Paraguay: Law 24836.
- Convention on Nuclear Safety: Law 24776.
- Convention for Cooperation in the Framework of the Ibero-American Conference: Law 24708.
- Statute of the Bi-National Managing Commission of the Lower Basin of the Pilcomayo River: Law 24697.
- Agreement for the Multiple Uses of the Resources of the Upper basin of the Bermejo River and Río Grande of Tarija, signed with Bolivia: Law 24639.
- Convention for Biological Diversity: Law 24375.
- Amendment to the Montreal Protocol on Substances that Deplete the Ozone Layer: Law 24418.
- United Nations Framework Convention on Climate Change: Law 24295.
- International Convention on Cooperation, Preparation and Response against Contamination by Hydrocarbons: Law 24292.
- Protocol on Environmental Protection to the Antarctic Treaty: Law 24216.
- Amendment to the Montreal Protocol on Substances that Deplete the Ozone Layer: Law 24167.
- Treaty with Chile on Environment: Law 24105.
- Convention on the Conservation of Migratory Species of Wild Animals: Law 23918.
- Convention on Wetlands of International Importance, RAMSAR: Law 23919.
- Agreement on Cooperation on Marine Environment Contamination by Hydrocarbons: Law 23829.
- Vienna Convention for the Protection of the Ozone Layer: Law 23724.
- Treaty Banning Nuclear Weapons Tests in the Atmosphere: Law 23340.
- Convention for the Conservation of Antarctic Marine Living resources: Law 22584.
- United Nations Convention on the Law of the Sea: Law 24543.
- Convention on International Trade of Endangered Species, Wild Flora and Fauna: Law 22344.
- Convention on the Prevention of Marine Pollution by Dumping of Waste and Other Materials: Law 21947.
- Treaty on the Río de la Plata and its Marine Front: Law 20645.
- Agreement on the Preservation of the Vicuña: Law 19282.
- Rio de La Plata Basin Treaty: Law 18590.

II. National Sources of Environmental Law

67. Following Gèny's thoughts, as masterfully explained by Llambías, 'lawyers must follow two legal expression sources: *formal sources*, to wit, legislation, customs and the appellate court rulings; and *material sources*, to wit, case law, doctrine, equity and comparative law.'[34]

68. As far as we are concerned, in the analysis of national environmental law sources, it is better to follow the practical importance criterion to figure out a fair solution for the case under study. Therefore, we will mention them in the following order of priority: legislation, case law, legal doctrine, usages and customary rules.

69. In Argentina following Professor Mario F. Valls' work, which constitutes a great effort to systematize the environmental law in the country[35] the following legal provisions shall be considered national environmental law sources: the civil, criminal and mining codes, together with the NC Furthermore, there are specific laws, particularly the General Environmental Law 25675 of 2002, the law on hydrocarbons and the different laws regulating other issues and including environmental provisions, such as, water law, labour laws, laws on vegetable and animal health, and laws on human health, disturbing noises and other national legislation.[36]

70. Case law as a means to reach fair environmental regulations can be traced back to the first Argentine ruling on environment issued by the CSJN in 1887, when the highest court confirmed the prohibition against operating slaughterhouses in the city of Buenos Aires.[37]

71. Legal doctrine is represented by the work of scholars who write relevant legal books, many of which are quoted and mentioned in this work. Professor Valls points out that the main feature of the environmental legal doctrine is that 'not only do specialists on environmental law nourish legal doctrine, but constitutional, administrative, criminal and civil lawyers and barristers and lawyers also cooperate' on the grounds that 'practically all legal fields have been influenced by the new environmental concern'.[38]

72. Usages and customary rules as a source of private law are specifically governed by Article 17 of the Civil Code, which states that 'customs and usage cannot

34. Jorge Joaquín Llambías, *Tratado de Derecho Civil: Parte General, 22ª Edición Actualizada por Patricio J. Raffo Benegas* (Buenos Aires: Abeledo Perrot, 2009), 1:45. Llambías explains that in 1925 F. Gèny in his work, *Método de Interpretación y Fuentes en Derecho Privado Positivo* made a distinction between formal and *scientific* sources of law. The latter was then called *material source* 'because it provides the issue itself or the law material object that is man's behaviour'.
35. Mario F. Valls, *Derecho Ambiental* (Buenos Aires: Abeledo Perrot 2008), 86.
36. As regards local environmental legislation as an environmental law source, Valls mentions procedural codes and local legislation on land-use planning, and other local environmental laws and codes.
37. Case *Podestá Santiago v. Provincia de Buenos Aires s/ Indemnización de daños y perjuicios*, National Supreme Court of Justice, Fallos, CXVIII, 278.
38. Valls, *supra*, 35, 107.

create rights, but only when the laws particularly refer to them or under non-legally governed circumstances'. That is why, as Cifuentes points out, customs accepted by the legal order (*secundum legem*) and customary rules to fill the gaps (*praeter legem*) 'are compulsory according to Article 17 of the Civil Code'. However, custom 'contrary to law, also called desuetude, does not repeal any law but makes it lose its efficacy'.[39] Valls explains that those customary rules are very common in environmental law and are usually beneficial for those who follow custom. However, they can be harmful for the rest of the community or future generations'.[40]

39. Santos Cifuentes (dir), *Código Civil Comentado y Anotado*, 2° Updated and extended edition (Buenos Aires: La Ley, 2008), 1:26. Room D of the National Court of Appeals on Civil matters has stated that 'Custom shall be applied even at the judge's decision without the need of evidence' (CNCiv, Sala D, 22.02.72, ED41-668).
40. *Idem* quotation 38.

Part I. Pollution Control

§1. Introduction

73. To begin with the explanation of this subject, we would like to note that Professor Steven Ferrey analyses the concepts of ethics and efficiency under the moral basis of pollution control, and considers that '[e]nvironmental protection laws have been enacted to further two primary goals: preventing irreparable environmental damage and forcing the consideration of environmental values into all realms of private and commercial activities'.[41]

74. It is also interesting to remind, as Professor Linda Malone sharply explains when she describes the methods of environmental regulation, that:

> [t]here are *three main approaches* to providing protection for the environment: A. Imposed controls: The government can protect the environment by *dictating amounts or methods* of controlling pollution', ... 'B. Market incentives: The government may use market forces to induce private organizations to reduce pollution to the levels that they find economically desirable' and 'C. Information disclosure: a third approach to protecting the environment is the requirement that *information* be produced about *the effects* of an action. The publication of information about the facility's action may influence the facility to choose a less harmful alternative.[42,43]

41. Steven Ferrey, *Environmental Law* 5 (4th ed., Aspen Publishers Wolters Kluwer Law & Business 2007). Bolds are in the original version.
42. Linda A. Malone, *Environmental Law*. Emanuel® Law Outlines C1-C2 (Aspen Publishers, Wolters Kluwer Law & Business 2007). In the original text some words are bold.
43. As it is noted by Blackman, developing countries [Argentina belongs to that category] are usually facing 'funding and guidance from multilateral and bilateral aid agencies, [and] are increasingly experimenting with alternative pollution control strategies that do not depend directly on regulators to issue mandates, monitor compliance, and sanction violations. Instead, they seek to leverage "informal" non regulatory pressures for environmental quality—including those applied by communities, capital markets, and consumers—and to lower the costs of pollution control and prevention. The best-known strategies of this type are public disclosure programs that collect and disseminate information about polluting facilities' environmental performance, and voluntary policies that invite polluters to commit to reducing their emissions'. Allen Blackman, *Alternative Pollution Control Policies in Developing Countries*. Symposium: Environmental Quality and Economic Development. (Review of Environmental Economics and Policy, 4, no. 2, Summer 2010): 234–253. Downloaded from www.oxfordjournals.org on 1 Nov. 2011. Also Percival et al. expose the different approaches to environmental problems and their implications, analysing from the 'environmental philosophy' to the 'relations between economics and the environment', the 'ecological perspectives', the 'myth of

And ever more, a recent study by Purdy proposes that earth observation technologies have a great opportunity to contribute to environmental control.[44]

75. As we hope to demonstrate throughout this text, Argentina has adopted the first and second methods for pollution control. Clearly, the third method works in societies where environmental conscience and information have higher levels of acceptance and voluntary fulfilment. Regrettably, that is not the general situation in Argentina yet.

---

the balance of nature' and the 'common pool resources' (derived from Garrett Hardin's famous *tragedy of the commons*). See Robert V. Percival et al., *Environmental Regulation: Law, Science and Policy* 15–59 (5th ed., Aspen Publishers – A Wolters Kluwer Business 2006).

44. Mentioned author considers that '[w]eaknesses in conventional mechanisms of implementation and enforcement of environmental laws, coupled with pressures to develop smarter and more resource-efficient regulatory approaches, suggest that there are real opportunities for the greater use of earth observation (EO) technologies as a regulatory compliance tool in environmental law. Technological improvements in the capabilities of satellites and associated EO technologies mean these could become increasingly relevant for those working in the environmental law sector'. Ray Purdy, '*Using Earth Observation Technologies for Better Regulatory Compliance and Enforcement of Environmental Laws*', *J. Environmental L.* 22, no. 1 (2010): 59–87. Downloaded from www.jel.oxfordjournals.org on 4 Jun. 2011.

Chapter 1. General Law

§1. Environmental Impact Assessment and Strategic Environmental Assessment (SEA)

I. General Remarks

76. In order to analyse the topic of the Environmental Impact Assessment (EIA), we must start highlighting that we find in the Oklahoma University Professor Larry W. Canter one of the most complete works[45] and – above all – useful for practical ends to any professional involved in an EIA, due to its clarity regarding the different technical criteria and possible methodologies therein explained.

77. In Argentina, Grassetti is the only jurist to write a book analysing EIAs from a legal point of view.

We will refer to both authors' teachings below, and then we will analyse the scope of Law 25675 of 2002 containing few Articles on this important environmental management instrument.

II. Environmental Impact Assessment (EIA)

78. To understand the EIA, it is significant to note – and extremely didactic – what Canter explains about *screening* activities in this process.[46] Said author points out that:

> *screening* and *scoping* are English terms that have been taken to be used in the EIA processes carried out in many countries. There are some subtle but also significant differences of how they are used in each and every of these countries. In fact, these terms are extensions of the idea of establishing how significant an impact is, a concept that has been described before

and he keeps on pointing out:

> [t]hen the fundamental topic within *screening* is that whether a complete environmental impact survey (or environmental assessment) must be carried out or not. The *scoping* focuses on determining the specific issues and impacts that need to be dealt with in the comprehensive environmental impact assessment survey. The *scoping* is normally presented after an affirmative decision on the necessity of carrying out a comprehensive impact assessment has been taken, although it can also be part of the considerations when the *screening* is carried out. In order to define whether a comprehensive environmental impact assessment survey should be carried out for a specific situation there exist two

45. Larry W. Canter, *Manual de Evaluación de Impacto Ambiental: Técnicas para la Elaboración de los Estudios de Impacto*, 2nd edn (Madrid: McGraw-Hill Interamericana de España S.A.U., 1998).
46. Canter, *supra*, 24 et seq.

different approaches: (a) the application of a category classification based on the types and sizes of the projects and, (b) a preliminary survey.

79. Eduardo Grassetti carefully deals with the different aspects of the EIA process in which a lawyer intervenes being of paramount importance the holistic approach of said author vis-à-vis the lawyer's involvement in the surveys of every EIA process.[47,48]

80. EIAs in Argentina were pioneered by the Buenos Aires province. According to provincial legislation, all the provinces require to conduct an EIA before issuing permits to carry out activities that may cause relevant negative impact to the environment or its resources. In many relevant projects supported by the World Bank or the Inter-American Development Bank environmental pre-feasibility and feasibility studies must be provided.

81. At the national level and according to Law 25675 of 2002 it is compulsory to carry out an EIA previous to any work or activity 'that may be prone to degrading the environment in a significant way' and whose elements may affect or alter the quality of life of the population.[49]

For further considerations regarding EIA at the federal level in Argentina, see §2 of this chapter.

82. In the province of Buenos Aires, the EIA is ruled by Law 11723 of 1995 which defines it as 'the process aimed to identify and interpret as well as to prevent the consequences or effects that public or private actions or projects may cause to the ecological balance, to the quality of life maintenance and to the preservation of the existing natural resources'.[50]

Said assessment was considered of paramount importance in a recent judicial case that involved the port of Mar del Plata (province of Buenos Aires) due to the presumed damage that works for tender would cause, in particular, to migrants

47. Eduardo R Grassetti, *Estudios Ambientales* (Buenos Aires: Publishing House Heliasta, 1998), 267–270 and 439–528. The profit of this complete work lies in that it not only studies the professional involvement for a lawyer in environmental audits according to ISO 14001 norms and IRAM norms, but also it comprises a very ample spectrum of commercial activities making reference to the environmental legal aspects that rule them, for example, the joint regulation passed by the national Port Authority and the SAyDS related to the environmental aspects that must be complied with so as to authorize a port in Argentina. Besides, this work makes reference to those regulations where the applying norm is national, or of the province of Buenos Aires (e.g., Law 11549 of Industrial Authorization) or – then – of the municipality of the city of Buenos Aires (in the latter case, it would require an update, due to the change in the juridical *status* observed, as a result of the reform of the National Constitution in 1994 by which the name 'Municipality of Buenos Aires' changed to 'Government of the Autonomous City of Buenos Aires)'.
48. For further developments and a technical approach to the concept of 'risk communication' we recommend the document elaborated by UERA in September 2010 titled *Comunicaciones de Riesgo: Una Aproximación Conceptual* where the notions of environmental risk, health environment and perception of risk, and the principal aspects of a Communications Plan, among others, are developed.
49. Article 11 of Law 25675 of 2002.
50. Appendix I of the law of the province of Buenos Aires 11723.

birds. As Prof. Esaín points out[51] the case fostered the federal competence and the Federal Court No. 2 of Mar del Plata sentenced:

> considering that, on the other hand, the work to be done by the Regional Port Consortium of Mar del Plata is of administrative nature, in the province of Buenos Aires territory, whose police power it reserves, then the national Law 25675 of 2002 shall be enforced (as of the date of its sentence which is subsequent to the tender date and for future activities in the same port, as well). Also, the Buenos Aires provincial Law 11723 of 1995 shall be enforced regarding full applicability in the proceedings (Articles 10 and 23)

and definitely considering that:

> the Regional Port Consortium of Mar del Plata has infringed the law at the time of the opening on November 11th 2002, of the Presentation of Bases and Conditions of Proposals for the beaches' exploitation within the port of Mar del Plata's jurisdiction, neighbouring with the wetland named Reserva Natural Puerto Mar del Plata in which some bird species observed ... nest during their migrant transit, without carrying out the previous Procedure of Environmental Impact Assessment indicated by Article 2 of Appendix II of Law 11723.

83. In the jurisdiction of the city of Buenos Aires, local Law 123 of 1998 applies as modified by Law 452 of 2000 and Law 1733 of 2005 ruled by Decree 1352 of 2002 which regulates the process of EIA and its stages for certain industrial enterprises. Mentioned law defines EIA and EI (Environmental Impact). The EIA is defined as the technical and administrative procedure for the identification and interpretation as well as the prevention of the short, intermediate and long-term effects that activities, projects, programmes or public or private enterprises may cause to the environment in terms of the aims set by this law. At the same time, Environmental Impact is understood as any net change either positive or negative that is brought about on the environment as a direct or indirect consequence of anthropogenic actions that may produce alterations prone to affect health and quality of life, the productive capacity of natural resources and essential ecological processes. This local norm is applicable to every activity, project, programmes or enterprise prone to bring about an environmental impact of relevant effect that may be carried out by any individuals, public or private artificial person.

III. Strategic Environmental Assessment (SEA)

84. The SEA has become an important planning instrument in the European Union for agriculture, forestry, fisheries, energy, industry, transport, waste management, water management, telecommunications, tourism and town and

51. José Alberto Esaín, *Competencias Ambientales* (Buenos Aires: Abeledo Perrot, 2008), 780–781. The case is *Fundación Reserva Natural Puerto Mar del Plata v. Consorcio Portuario Regional de Mar del Plata s Amparo Ambiental* and the sentence dates back to 26 Dec. 2002.

country planning or land-use, where a SEA Directive has been approved in 2001. In Argentina SEA regulations are still being studied, analysed and discussed. Recent developments have been produced at the jurisdictional level of the city of Buenos Aires. We will shortly refer to both situations in the next two paragraphs.

85. Explaining what SEA is and how it works in the European Union, particularly in England, Wooley et al. wrote that:

> [i]n a similar fashion to planning applications, the environmental consequences of certain plans and other projects will need to be assessed prior to their adoption or implementation. Those 'plans and projects' will be subject to review to ensure that they '... provide for a high level of protection of environmental considerations into the preparation and adoption of plans and programmes with a view to promoting sustainable development'. This requirement is now set out in the Environmental Assessment of Plans and Programmes Regulations 2004. These Regulations implement Directive 2001/42/EC, commonly known as the Strategic Environmental Assessment Directive. This had to be implemented in the UK by 21 July 2004, and although the UK Government failed to do so in time, this does not appear to have had any significant consequences in the long run.[52]

86. Exclusively for the city of Buenos Aires' jurisdiction, the local government introduced the so-called Strategic Plan Buenos Aires 2010, which comprises the SEA as a strategic planning tool for the sustainable development of said city. This document defines the SEA as 'a systemic process by which the environmental impact considerations are set up for every policy, plan or programme that is at the project stage.' The SEA is a management tool that makes possible the incorporation of urban-environmental consideration at the pre-project level of the decision-making, in the formulation and execution of specific policies, plans and programmes of the public management. Differences between EIA and SEA are expressly set up when affirming that:

> [1] the SEA will have an impact on the future scenarios either mitigating the negative effects or boosting the opportunity conditions of the urban space. Unlike EIA passed by Law 123 plus its modified Law, the SEA does not analyze minimum impact magnitudes but global impacts.[53]

---

52. David Wooley QC et al., *Environmental Law* 708–710 (2d ed., Oxford U. Press 2009). Chapter 15 of this extraordinary book is devoted to EIA, explaining the authors that 'the agreement at Kiev of the Protocol on SEA to the Espoo Convention (May 2003) may lead to further reforms to the sea requirements in due course'. *Supra* n. 11, at 708.

53. *Evaluación Ambiental Estratégica.* Plan Estratégico Buenos Aires 2010, 11. On internet: www.metropolitana.org.ar/archivo/prensa/informes_especiales/eae.pdf (accessed 17 Oct. 2011). Recently, the 'Strategic Plan Buenos Aires 2016 was introduced: With Metropolitan Perspective'. On internet: www.espacio-abierto.org.ar/imageneslubertino/documentos/planestrategicobuenosaires 2016.pdf (accessed 19 Oct. 2011).

IV. EIA and the ICJ Decision on the Pulp Mills Case *Argentina v. Uruguay*

87. In 2005, Uruguay authorized the Finnish company 'Botnia' to construct -on the banks of the Uruguay River- one of the largest pulp mills in the world. So began an international environmental dispute with Argentina who made a number of claims – including blockades of bridges between the two border countries – against mentioned act, basically on the grounds that Uruguay breached its obligation to notify and consult with Argentina *previously* to render the authorization, as established by the 1975 Statute of the River Uruguay. Negotiations failed so Argentina finally submitted in 2006 its dispute to the International Court of Justice (ICJ) along with a request for provisional measures.

88. As Pietter H.F. Bekker has explained '[t]he key point of contention between the parties is whether or not the pulp mills would comply with international norms regarding effluent emission'.[54]

89. Accordingly, Payne wrote that:

> [o]n both sides of the river, citizens worried about dioxin, furan, and other pulp plant pollutants harming fish, birds, honeybees, and fruit crops. In Uruguay, many argued that they needed the jobs and export income from the pulp mills, but on the Argentine side of the river people expected no economic benefit from the mills and feared harm to agriculture and tourism.[55]

Mentioned author also explains that the ICJ:

> found that the 1975 Statute defines Uruguay's substantive obligations, consistent with the principles of pollution prevention and cooperation that it invoked in the Gabcíkovo-Nagymaros case and the Legality of the Threat or Use of Nuclear Weapons advisory opinion. The Court called on both parties to coordinate their regulatory activities to preserve the ecological balance of the river, as required by Article 36 of the 1975 Statute. The role of CARU in coordination and rulemaking was particularly relevant here, reflecting the common interest expressed in the 1975 Statute.

And concludes observing that:

> [t]he Court observed that the practice of EIA has gained so much acceptance among States that it may now be considered a requirement under general international law to undertake an EIA where there is a risk that the proposed

54. Pieter H.F. Bekker, *Argentina-Uruguay Environmental Border Dispute Before the World Court*. ASIL Insights, 16 May 2006, vol. 10, no. 11. On the internet: www.asil.org/insights060516.cfm (accessed 13 Mar. 2011).

55. Cymie R. Payne, *Pulp Mills on the River Uruguay: The International Court of Justice Recognizes that Environmental Impact Assessment as a Duty under International Law*. American Society of International Law (ASIL) Insight, 22 Apr. 2010, vol. 14, no. 9. Accessible on the internet: www.asil.org/ insights100422.cfm (accessed 13 Mar. 2011).

> industrial activity may have a significant adverse impact in a transboundary context, in particular, on a shared resource.

In this case, the 1975 Statute did not require an EIA, but the parties agreed that an EIA was needed.

One cannot disagree with Payne's argument that:

> [t]his judgment is a significant step forward in the ICJ's jurisprudence on environmental law and on shared watercourses. The Court recognized environmental impact assessment as a practice that has become an obligation of general international law in these situations. It further found that general international law does not prescribe the scope or content of such assessments.

§2. Environmental Permits

90. At the federal level, any work or activity that may cause significant negative effects on the environment is subject to an EIA *previous* to the activity be accomplished, as it is set forth by Articles 11–13 of Law 25675 of 2002.[56]

91. Most environmental laws also establish permits for the operation of industries, discharge of wastewaters, air emissions and hazardous waste management. They may be transferred together with the ownership of the plant or facility.

92. The EIA is an administrative procedure that begins with an affidavit in which it must be declared if the activities to be developed will affect, or not, the environment. The competent authorities have to issue an administrative act: the so-called Declaration of Environmental Impact (DEI),[57] which has one of three possible contents: an acceptance of the project, its rejection, or the modifications that need to be introduced to the studies already presented.

93. The environmental studies to be presented must contain, at least, a detailed description of the project to be developed, the identification of its environmental consequences (impacts) and the actions to be carried out in order to mitigate the negative effects on the environment.

94. Contrary to what is established by some provincial rules, the federal Law 25675 does not provide for enforcement measures for violations of the conditions taken into account to issue a permit.

56. Article 11 of the LGA states: 'Any work or action that in the National Territory shall be capable of degrading the environment or any of its components or affecting population lifestyle in a significant way will be subjected to an environmental assessment procedure before its execution.'
57. Which is mandatory according to the provisions set forth by Art. 12 of Law 25675 of 2002.

§3. The Right to a Healthy Environment

95. In the Florence Conference organized in 2004 by the European Society of International Law (ESIL) Nicole Bjerler presented a paper containing a deep study of the interrelationship between human rights and the environment. Mentioned author highlighted the emergence of a human right to the environment in the European context and concluded that 'yes, there is wide-spread recognition of procedural rights to environment. The Aarhus Convention has established an explicit link between human rights and the environment that can no longer be denied or ignored by States'.[58]

96. This approach, according to which environmental rights are human rights, is parallel with the argument for which violations of environmental duties are human rights violations. It is one of the actual concerns of the international public law, as it was pointed out in a very recent study by Olawuyi published by Oxford University Press.[59]

97. In Argentina, there are also many authors for whom the right to the environment is a human right.[60]

---

58. That author also points out that 'even though international environmental law has the potential to substantially contribute to the improvement of the global environment, it generally does not provide individuals with enforceable rights. Does this leave human beings entirely defenceless in the eve of environmental deterioration? One way to alter our collective harmful behaviour may be to vest individuals with a right to environment and thereby give the victims of environmental degradation a clear voice. Such a human right to environment would supplement traditional international environmental law and empower human beings in their quest for a sustainable and healthy environment'. Nicole Bjerler, *Do Europeans Have a Right to Environment?* This 'Agora' paper presented at the 2004 Florence Founding Conference of the ESIL was published by the European Journal of International Law (EJIL) later, and is available online at www.esil-sedi.eu/english/florence_agora_ papers.html (accessed 28 Mar. 2009).
59. See Damilola S. Olawuyi, *Adopting the Language of Rights for Environmental Protection: Legal and Theoretical Justifications* (Oxford: Oxford Student Legal Studies Paper No. 11/2011, 21 Oct. 2011), where the author sustains that 'One of the current debates in public international law is the question of whether to treat environmental violations as human rights violations. These debates have been developed in a fragmented manner by different scholars, theorists and thinkers in the field of public international law.' This paper takes the analysis further; it reviews, analyses and responds to the legal and theoretical debates surrounding the proposals for the creation and recognition of a substantive environmental right under international law. It considers the questions 'why do we need an environmental right under international law and can environmental protection be rightly classified as a human right concern?' The debates are explored under two headings: the proliferation debate (the new right will lead to a proliferation and devaluation of the human rights currency); and the redundancy debate (the new right will be redundant as environmental concerns are already indirectly covered by existing human rights treaties, common law remedies and environmental agreements). Full text of this article is readable at http://ssrn.com/abstract=1947545 (accessed 24 Oct. 2011).
60. Marcelo Alberto López Alfonsín y Carlos Eduardo Tambussi, 'El medio ambiente como derecho humano', in *Derechos Humanos*, 5th edn, ed. Agustín Gordillo (Buenos Aires: Fundación de Derecho Administrativo, 1999) In internet: www.gordillo.com/Pdf/DH--5/Capitulo_XIII.pdf (accessed 27 Sep. 2010).

98. In particular, the right to a 'healthy' environment is one of the main innovative rules introduced in the country's legal system by the 1994 national Constitutional amendment.[61] It is set forth in a new section of the NC named 'New Rights and Guarantees' within which Article 41 states:

> Every inhabitant has the right to have a healthy environment, suitable for human development and for productive activities to satisfy the current needs without jeopardizing that of the future generations; and it has the duty to preserve it. The environmental damage will firstly generate the obligation to repair, according to the law.

99. By expressly incorporating in Article 41 of the NC the right of all the inhabitants to an 'environment that is healthy, balanced, suitable for human development and for the productive activities to satisfy the current needs without neglecting those of the future generations', the 1994 reform makes the human development to be the aim of the environment preservation imposing limits on productive activity. That is similar to the criterion set by Article 4 of Law 25675 of 2002 which establishes the national environmental policy principles, to which we made reference in §2 of the Introduction when we referred to the basic principles of environmental law.

§4. Environmental Management within Companies

I. Introduction: Legal Framework

100. As Robert Percival et al. explain '[t]he increasing economic importance of multinational corporations has led to a growing interest in strategies that foster voluntary environmentalism by corporations. One approach seeks to build on the trend toward corporate environmental reports'. Said authors also explain that '[a]nother source or incentives for voluntary improvements in the environmental behaviour of private companies is through private standards developed by national and international-setting standards',[62] as the International Organization for Standardization (ISO) founded in 1947.

101. It is known that every country has its national standardization agency[63] where in general the observed evolution of the company environmental awareness

61. In short, the most innovative rules are related to: (i) the recognition of all the inhabitants' right to a 'healthy and balanced environment', (ii) the rule according to which the environmental damage brings about primarily an obligation to remediate 'according to what the law rules' (iii) the authorities' duty to take action in order to protect and enhance these rights and to promote the rational use of the natural resources, the biodiversity and the environmental information and education (iv) the attribution for national authorities to set forth the rules in order to establish the minimum standards for environmental protection, having the provinces been left with the duty to establish the 'complementary' rules to reinforce them, and (v) the prohibition against introducing present or potentially dangerous and radioactive waste into the Argentine territory.
62. Robert V. Percival et al., *Environmental Regulation: Law, Science and Policy* 1120 (5th ed., Aspen Publishers – A Wolters Kluwer Business, 2006).
63. Developing the concepts of 'eco-management' and 'eco-audit' Lorente Aznar explained in 1996:

is reflected, since the Bruntland Report introduced the concept of 'sustainable development' in 1987 up to the Rio Conference of 1992 when said concept was practically applied. Since then there was some warning that the environmental management norms, even though they were useful tools for corporate image, were poorly cleared and fundamentally that is credibility depended upon the company itself that implemented them. Then the certification by an independent third party was convenient. It was in 1992 when ISO was entrusted with the management tool study that would allow balancing the commerce and industry needs together with the compliance of environmental measures. ISO developed over 18,000 international standards on a variety of subjects, among which ISO 14000 Standards refer to environmental management. In particular, the ISO 14001:2004 addresses the requirements for an Environmental Management System (EMS), and the ISO 14004:2004 are devoted to the guidelines specially prepared for conducting an EMS.

102. In Argentina, Decree 1474 of 1994 creates the National System of Norms, Quality and Certification, which regulates the standardization and credentials within the strict voluntary field.[64] In said National System two agencies operate: the credentials agency (Argentine Institute of Standardization and Certification, IRAM)[65] and the certification agency (Argentine Agency of Credentials, OAA). Through said Decree the National Board of Norms, Quality and Certification is also created and the IRAM and OAA's functions are established. The IRAM is a member of ISO and its function is to centralize the study and adopt norms over which the whole national quality system is founded. The OAA is in charge of the certification agency's credentials and those of the test and calibration laboratories. The ISO 14001 was adopted in Argentina under the name of IRAM – ISO 14001 'Environmental Management Systems (EMS), Specifications and Directions for Use'. Also, IRAM adopted IRAM-ISO 14004 IRAM-ISO 14001 'Environmental Management Systems (EMS), General Guidelines on Principles, Systems and Support Techniques' whose general objective is to provide assistance for agencies to implement or enhance an EMS.

'[i]n the United States it is not something new the special attention that companies and multinational companies are paying to environment. Some rigid, strict norms to the contaminating companies have paved the way for a preventative development of an industrial production compatible with the environment. In Spain, the situation tends to get generalized together with that of other developed countries, mainly since the incorporation of our country to the European Union. The first sector to understand the need to have in mind some environmental policies in their productive processes has been the industrial sector.' César J. Lorente Aznar, *Empresa, Derecho y Medio Ambiente* (Barcelona: J.M. Bosch Editor S.A., 1996), 25.

64. Article 1 of Decree 1474 of 1994 creates said National System 'with the purpose of providing reliable tools at a national and international level for companies that voluntarily accept to certify the quality systems, products, services and processes through a mechanism that relies on the standardization, credential and certification agencies integrated with the international norms in force. The norms that derive from the created system will be of voluntary nature'.

65. The Argentine IRAM was created in 1935. It was the first institute of standardization in Latin America.

103. Particular liabilities may arise for those who manage or administer legal entities, as we will see in paragraph 493 of this work.

II. Sustainability Reports

104. The Argentine Corporate Board for the Sustainable Development (CEADS by its acronym in Spanish) gathers the main companies of the country. In 2005, it prepared some Guidelines for the Elaboration of Reports on Sustainability. Many of the big Argentine companies have drafted and published this kind of Reports, some of which are directly available on the website of mentioned Board.[66]

III. Eco-Labelling

105. In Argentina, and for some products as low voltage electric equipment, toys, security locking for the containers of hazardous products of domestic use, building concrete and steel, gas devices, among others, the IRAM adopted – through Resolution 799 of 1999 passed by the Secretariat of Industry, Commerce and Mining – a conformity brand 'S' that is to be granted when a product has been certified according to an IRAM rule and complies with the legal requirements demanded for its consideration as a safe product.

66. For example, the Annual Sustainability Report 2009/10 of the Argentine agro-industrial group Ledesma (made with paper of sugar cane by said company) has the virtue of presenting the table of indicators of Guideline G3 of the Global Reporting Initiative (GRI-Global Reporting Initiative) where the report pages are shown in which the indicators are featured. In this Report, said group highlights that 'we show our commitment with the 10 principles of the World Pact of United Nations and we comply with the elaboration of Communications on Progress (COP) for 2010'. For more detailed information please go to www.globalreporting.org and www.pactoglobal.org.ar. See www.ceads.org.ar. Due to reasons we ignore, it is not available via internet. (14 Nov. 2011).

Chapter 2. Air Pollution

§1. General

106. As Tyler Miller Jr. points out '[w]e live at the bottom of the "sea" of air called the atmosphere.[67] This thin envelope of life-sustaining gases surrounding the earth is divided into several spherical layers characterized by abrupt changes in temperature, the result of differences in the absorption of incoming solar energy'.[68] Putting it clearly, as mentioned author usually does, he expresses that an 'air pollutant is a chemical in the wrong place in the wrong concentration' and that they may be classified in primary and secondary pollutants and that the 'major classes of air pollutants' are carbon oxides, sulphur oxides, nitrogen oxides, volatile organic compounds, suspended particles, photochemical oxidants, radioactive substances and toxic compounds'.[69]

In this work we will only refer to air pollution 'in the open air', which opposes to the so-called indoor air pollution. The latter falls under the scope of the health and occupational safety regulations applicable to labour environments inside workers' facilities, and is directly related to smoking bans and *tobacco free* buildings, among other policies.

§2. Specific Legislation

107. According to a study by the Natural Resources and Environment Foundation, 'regarding environmental regulations vis-à-vis air quality conservation, the member countries' regulations of the Treaty of Asunción [which created the MERCOSUR] are very limited'.[70] In Argentina, the atmospheric contamination is ruled by Law 20284 of 1973, which was passed by Congress and has three Appendices.[71] This law has not been ruled until today and it is complemented with two resolutions dictated by the National Department of Health, which establish the Health and Air Quality Programme[72] and the limits to the lead content in latex paint.[73] Among other innovations, this law also creates the Cadastral Registry of Contaminating Sources in the national sanitary authority's field.

67. The word 'atmosphere' is emphasized on the original text. George Tyler Miller Jr, *Living in the Environment: Principles, Connections and Solutions* 463 (10th ed., Wadsworth Publishing Company 1998).
68. *Ibid.*, 463.
69. *Ibid.*, 467.
70. See Ch. III, s. 5 of the report *Bases para la Armonización de Exigencias en el Mercosur*. Sine locus. Fundación Ambiente y Recursos Naturales FARN. Estudio Analítico N° 4, 1995. Promoted by W. Alton Jones Foundation (USA). On internet www.farn.org.ar/docs/p03/publicaciones33.html #mercosurIII-5. Visited 18 Nov. 2011.
71. Appendix I is applied to 'Cars with Motor by Spark Combustion', Appendix II states the air quality norms for the different contaminants, making a distinction between three situations: 'Alert, Alarm and Emergency' and the sample methods/analysis for the contaminants CO, NOx, SO_2, O3 and oxidants, suspended particles and sedimentary particles. Appendix III has a series of definitions.
72. Resolution 638 of 2001 of the National Health Department.
73. Resolution 1088 of 2004 of the then called Environment and Health Department.

108. The national, provincial and city of Buenos Aires Sanitary Authority in their respective jurisdictions are the enforcing authorities of this regime. For the inter-jurisdictional contamination cases, the enforcing authority with the purpose of applying and supervising this regime is the Inter-Jurisdictional Committee created by Chapter V of this law, whose main function is to evaluate the current situation and set norms of emission suitable for the zone's characteristics.[74]

109. This regime empowers the national sanitary authority to structure and run a national programme related to the causes, effects, scopes and methods to prevent atmospheric pollution.

110. The national sanitary authority is expressly entitled[75] to set norms regarding air quality and contaminant concentration. This law also entitles the national Executive Power to modify the values set in Appendix I and II whenever necessary.

111. Likewise, the local sanitary authorities are also entitled to set the maximum emission levels of the different fixed sources for every zone under each jurisdiction, to declare and supervise the compliance of the prevention plan of critical situations of atmospheric pollution with the exceptions mentioned on the third Article of this law 20284 of 1973. Regarding the fixed sources of existent contamination at the date of this law, it was stipulated that terms would be fixed so as to adapt the contaminant emissions to inferior levels against the allowed maximums.

112. The offences to this regime are set in Chapter IV of this law and pave the way for sanctions application which range from fines (from ARS 100 up to ARS 50000), temporary or final closing of the contaminating source and temporal or final disqualification of the circulation permit. In case of recidivism, penalties increase.

113. The legal action has a limitation period of two years from the date when the offence was committed. The limitation period is interrupted should another offence be committed.

114. In the city of Buenos Aires' jurisdiction, Law 1356 of 2004 is applicable. It was adopted by the legislative body of said city, which is applicable to every public or private source capable of producing atmospheric pollution in said city, coordinating the inter-jurisdictional and inter-institutional ones without affecting what was established by Law 20284 of 1973.[76] This local norm states, among other things, the atmospheric quality standards and the emission limits for the city of Buenos Aires.

74. The functions of the Inter-Jurisdictional Committee are ruled by Art. 22 of this law.
75. Article 6 of Law 20284 of 1973.
76. Article 3 of said law defines atmospheric contamination as 'the direct or indirect introduction, through human activity, of substances or energies into the atmosphere which may produce deleterious effects for the human health or for the environment quality or that may cause damage to material goods or deteriorate or impede the enjoyment or other lawful uses of the environment'.

115. The enforcing Authority[77] is entitled with the obligation of setting the sample and analysis methods of the atmospheric contaminants, permanent monitoring programmes, prevention plans and atmospheric pollution correction and the make-up of an inventory of fixed sources of emission, with its geographic distribution and current relevant data, on a yearly basis. Likewise, the enforcing Authority is expressly entitled to update the lists by national legislation, related to the ozone layer depleting substances. For those transit-related mobile sources, the 'emission limits of the international norm of integration and the national norms related to mobile sources' are adopted.[78]

77. Environmental Protection Agency of the Buenos Aires city.
78. Article 30 of this law. The gaseous emissions regime applicable to car transport of passengers which circulate the city of Buenos Aires is established by Resolution 114 of 2010 passed by the Environmental Protection Agency of the city of Buenos Aires.

Chapter 3. Water Pollution

§1. Introduction

116. The importance of water for Humanity as a whole has increased in recent years not only because the Earth is composed by 70% of that vital element – notwithstanding the wrong name given to our planet – but also because of its scarcity and the uses societies make of it.

117. Recent studies show that 400 to 500 million people lack of potable water and predictions are even worse: if no proper measures are taken thereof and the actual demographic growth follows the same it is expected that among 1,200 and 1,500 million people will suffer from water scarcity in the year 2025.

118. It is also interesting to note that water resources may be internationally considered a 'right' or a 'commodity' as it was left clear during the proceedings of the World Forum on Water (Kyoto 2003) and its parallel meetings that took place in Florence, Italy.[79]

119. Besides, it is often spoken of 'virtual water' as the volume of water used to produce a commodity or service. In 2000, a research, studying the strategic importance and implications of soil water – also called 'green water' – in relation to international crop trade, was conducted. The importance of green water comes from the fact that it is considered more sustainable than the use of 'blue water' which is the one that comes from irrigation. A recent research carried out by Aldaya, Hoekstra and Allan's corroborates that most global crop production is rain-fed, and concludes that during the period 2000–2004 green water was the largest share of virtual water embodied in maize, soybean and wheat exports from Argentina in addition to the USA, Canada and Australia.[80]

120. Argentina 'has an annual average water offer per inhabitant highly satisfactory, superior to the 26,000 m^3/inhab'.[81] Said distribution is very irregular by observing 'the different geographic climates and regions'. In fact, the sub-humid, semi-arid and arid areas represent 75% of the total country's surface. Among them, there exist the Chaco region, the Puna region, the Arid Valleys region, the centrewest and the Patagonia region. The largest water system is the Río de la Plata basin, which holds

79. Roberto Bloch, 'El Valor del Agua Dulce en la Supervivencia de la Humanidad', in *Agenda Internacional Nº 5* s/l (sine locus) 1. www.agendainternacional.com/numerosAnteriores/n5/ 0507.pdf. 18 May 2010.
80. M.M. Aldaya et al., 'Strategic Importance of Green Water in International Crop Trade', in *Value of Water Research Report Series Nº 25*, UNESCO-IHE Institute for Water Education, Delft, the Netherlands in collaboration with University of Twente, Enschede, the Netherlands and Delft University of Technology, Delft, the Netherlands. March 2008. www.unesco-ihe.org/.../ Report25-Green WaterInInternationalTrade.pdf. 18 Sep. 2009.
81. INCyTH/UNESCO, 'Balance hídrico de la República Argentina', (INCyTH/UNESCO, 1994). As quoted by Lilian del Castillo, *La Gestión del Agua en Argentina* (Buenos Aires: Ciudad Argentina, 2007), 43, n. 37.

85% of the average total spill and which, due to its richness, is the region that concentrates population, urban development and economic activity the most. This basin is made up of the Pilcomayo, Bermejo, Paraná, Paraguay, Iguazú and Uruguay,[82] rivers' sub-basins and others that extend over their neighbouring countries' territories.

121. In the Atlantic slope, there are the Río de la Plata Basin and other water systems coming from The Andes while 'regarding the Pacific slope, its water system reaches a great volume in the thaw time'.[83]

122. According to mentioned hydrological characteristics, the country is divided into four hydro-geological regions: (i) the Intermontane Valley Region which covers Cuyo and the North-west including the provinces of Jujuy, Salta, Tucumán, Catamarca, La Rioja, San Juan, San Luis and Mendoza all having arid and semi-arid climate; (ii) the Region of the Chaco-Pampeana Plains, which includes de provinces of Formosa, Chaco, Corrientes, Santa Fe, Entre Ríos, Santiago del Estero, Córdoba, La Pampa, Buenos Aires and CABA, where the 'Puelche' aquifer is located; (iii) the Region of the Misiones Plateau, which includes the Province of Misiones and part of Corrientes and forms part of the mega-aquifer 'Guarani' that links Brazil, Paraguay, Uruguay and Argentina and; (iv) the Region of the Patagonian Plateaus, which extends from Tierra del Fuego to the Colorado River and includes the provinces of Neuquen, Rio Negro, Chubut, Santa Cruz and Tierra del Fuego.[84]

123. The legal regime on waters includes surface, glacial and ground ones. Surface and ground waters rules are mainly established in the Civil Code and glacial water rules have been recently established by Law 25688 of 2002 on minimum environmental standards for the protection of water resources. We will dedicate a special paragraph to the rules and recently decided cases regarding glacial waters in §2 III of this chapter.

§2. Surface Water

I. General Rules

124. Regarding water uses, the most authorized doctrine has distinguished the common uses such as navigation and fishing (which are 'those that can be made by all men due to their condition as such and without any other prerequisite than the compliance of the regulation of general nature passed by the authority') and the special uses such as irrigation, being as such those that 'do not mainly and

82. *Ibid.*
83. del Castillo, *supra*, 44.
84. *Argentina Water Resources Management: Policy Issues and Notes Thematic Annexes* vol. 3, 25 Feb. 2000. 48.

immediately aim at meeting indispensable physical needs for life itself, but increasing the action sphere and the economic power of man'.[85]

125. According to Articles 2340 and 2341 of the Civil Code the territorial sea within a distance of twelve miles,[86] the interior seas, the harbours, the rivers, the beaches, the navigable lakes and all waters that may satisfy uses of general interest are 'public goods' which belong to the public property of the federal state or the provinces. Private people and landowners – should that be the case – have the right to use them according to the provisions of the Civil Code and the statutory rules approved thereof.[87]

126. Regarding water uses, the Civil Code establishes a series of significant rules such as the banning of the use of natural resources waters without the granting of the competent authority,[88] the inferior country states holders' 'obligation' of receiving the waters coming from superior country states (Articles 2647–2650) and the norms regarding water rights (Articles 3104–3107).

127. From the very beginning of its existence as a state, the throwing of industrial and household waste into navigable waters without a previous treatment was banned. Law 2797 of 1891 clearly established mentioned prohibition.

II. Pollution and Water Quality

128. The discharge-to-waters regime is governed by Decree 674 of 1989 as amended by Decree 776 of 1992.[89] This regime is applicable in the CABA and a

---

85. Ph.D. thesis recommended for the 'Facultad' Award, by the eminent Argentine academic and jurist Miguel S. Marienhoff, *Régimen y Legislación de las Aguas Públicas y Privadas* (Buenos Aires: Valerio Abeledo Editor, Librería Jurídica, 1939), 703–705, 728 et seq.
86. Article 3 of Law 23968 of 1991 establishes a twelve mile distance for the Argentine territorial sea, from the baselines.
87. Article 2340 of the Civil Code states: 'Among the public goods, there are: (1) territorial seas as far as determined by the special legislation, independent form the jurisdictional power over the adjoining zone; (2) inner seas, bays, inlets, ports and docs; (3) Rivers, their courses, the other water flowing in the natural courses and any other water that has or gets the characteristic to meet general interests uses, including underground waters, without detriment to the regular exercise of the owner to extract the underground waters according to his interests and complying with the laws.; (4) the beaches and inner banks of the rivers, understanding those as the extension that the waters touch or leave during the normal high tides or ordinary medium flooding; (5) navigable lakes and their beds; (6) the already formed island or the ones that get formed in the territorial sea or in any type of river or in the navigable lakes when they do not belong to individuals; (7) streets, squares, paths, channels, bridges or any other public work build up for common use or comfort; (8) the official documents of the branches of governments; (9) the ruins and archaeological and palaeontologist sites of scientific interests.'
88. Article 2642 of the Civil Code establishes it so by stating: 'For those who live by rivers, it is prohibited without special concession of the competent authority to change the natural course of waters, dig in their beds or extract them in any way or in any volume for their lands.'
89. Industrial, truck and car-washing facilities are included in the provisions of this regime according to Annex I of Resolution 25 of 2004 issued by SAyDS. In Argentina, the SAyDS establishes the standards for the effluents for the spilling in the industrial and special institutions, replacing those already set by the Nation Water Services Resolution 7917 of 1990.

number of local counties surrounding it, to the 'industrial' and 'special' facilities. Several definitions are provided by this rule, being the most important those of 'facility' 'industrial facility', 'special facility', 'permissible limit', 'limit temporarily tolerated' and 'limit of polluting pondered total charge'. It is derived to the SAyDS to establish and modify the limits based on the 'guide values for watercourses'. Industrial facilities are defined as those establishments that manufacture or transform raw material into new goods. Special facilities are defined as those that clean or process goods without transforming raw material.

129. According to this regime, it is mandatory to file an annual affidavit providing information to the SAyDS on the discharged pollutants.

130. Article 12 establishes the prohibition against accumulating solid and semisolid waste, substances notwithstanding their nature or characteristics and, where they are placed, if they constitute or may constitute a danger of pollution to the surface or ground waters. Should a facility bear these kinds of pollutants, then all the incurred costs for their removal, transportation, treatment and final deposition have to be supported by the facility and without prejudice of the sanctions provided in this regime.

131. Article 14 bans the following actions: (i) discharge effluents without the previous permit issued by the SAyDS, exception made for the home ones, (ii) discharge non-tolerated effluents, (iii) discharge effluents directly or indirectly to public areas and ground waters, (iv) mislead, hide information or not to present the annual affidavit to the SAyDS, (v) not to fulfil this regime or the statutory rules approved thereof.

132. The enforcement actions consist on fines and, in some cases, penal actions against the offender. Fines procedures may be suspended if the defendant provides satisfactory financial warranties. Any person is entitled to denounce illegal discharges on water corps and is also entitled to render proof of his allegations. He may act even verbally but it is mandatory to record his personal data for identification.

133. This regime also establishes a Special Right for Pollution Control (SRPC). It is a tax collected by the SAyDS and due by those facilities whose effluents hold a concentration of pollutants superior to the limits established by the applicable rules. There is a waiver procedure for the SRPC that consists of rendering proof that the facility has taken the necessary steps to enhance their spilling quality to permissible limits. This waiver period may last no more than thirty months. Should this period elapse and the facility's effluents not be according the limits set forth, the SAyDS is entitled to collect the waived taxes plus interest.

III. Environmental Preservation of Glaciers and Periglacial Regions

134. Glaciers constitute water resources reserves of paramount importance and are indicators of the climate change. As the document elaborated by the Argentine

Institute of Nivology, Glaciers and Environmental Sciences (IANIGLIA as per its acronym in Spanish) goes: 'Argentina is one of the few countries in the world that has some thousand square kilometres of glaciers and Permafrost Mountain in its territory.'

135. According to some approximated calculations, South America:

> would have about 25500 km^2 covered by glaciers with a 75% of the total area located in Chile (Williams and Ferrigno 1999; UNEP 2007). Our country comes second after Chile with around 15% of the total glaciers in South America. These percentages place both Chile and Argentina in a privileged position vis-à-vis other countries but it also grants them a larger degree of responsibility for the study, monitoring and protection of glaciers in this region of the planet.[90]

The National Park 'Los Glaciares' in the Argentine Patagonia has been declared a common heritage of mankind by UNESCO.

136. Argentina has a specific minimum environmental standards regime for glacier and periglacial preservation: Law 26639 of 2010, which defines glaciers as 'a good of public character' and its regulatory Decree 207 of 2011.[91] Debates in the National Congress are developed among centralized controversies in the adverse environmental effects of the mining activities that use cyanide to separate the metal from the rock in the Andes. In its first version, the law had been passed in 2008 but it was totally vetoed by the national Executive Branch because the mining and oil activities banning were considered excessive in the glaciers. After the presidential veto, the national Congress in 2010 passed law 26639, which obliged the execution of a National Inventory of Glaciers by the IANIGLIA, dependent on the National Scientific and Technical Research Council (CONICET).

This norm also sets the execution of a survey of priority zones where there are industrial establishments and the obligation to conduct environmental audits, among other rules. The National Inventory of Glaciers[92] has not been done yet, despite the technical document that sets the bases and it was elaborated for such aim by the IANIGLIA in December 2010.[93]

---

90. *Inventario Nacional de Glaciares y Ambiente Periglacial: Fundamentos y Cronología de Ejecución.* Instituto Argentino de Nivología, Glaciología y Ciencias Ambientales IANIGLIA – CONICET 2010, 3. Document available on internet: www.glaciares.org.ar/upload/CronogramaInventarioGlaciares IANIGLA.pdf (accessed 29 Oct. 2011).
91. At the same time, Art. 2 of Law 26639 defines a glacier as any mass of ice constant and stable that slowly flows with or without gap water, creating the new snow crystallization located in different ecosystems whatever their shape, dimension and conservation state. The detrital rocky material and the inner and superficial water courses are constitutive part. The periglacial environment in the high mountains is understood as that area with frozen soils that works as regulator of the water course. In the medium and los mountain the area that functions as water resources regulator with saturated soils in ice.
92. To October 2011.
93. *Inventario Nacional de Glaciares y Ambiente Periglacial: Fundamentos y Cronología de Ejecución.* IANIGLIA – CONICET 2010.

137. In the glaciers, activities prone to affect the natural conditions as well as those that imply the destruction or transferring or activities interfering with its progress are prohibited. Particularly, the following are prohibited: liberation, dispersion or disposition of pollutant substances or elements, chemical products or waste of any nature or volume; the construction of architecture work or infrastructure except those needed for scientific investigation and risk prevention; the mining and hydrocarbon exploration and exploitation and the installation of industries or development of industrial works or activities.

138. Forbidden activities are subjected to the previous EIA procedure in accordance to the General Law of the Environment 25675 of 2002.

139. The rescue, scientific and sporting activities are exempted from said requirements.

§3. GROUND WATER

I. Guarany Aquifer

140. Law 26780 of 2012 (published by the Official Gazzette on 23 November 2012) approved the international agreement on the Guaraní Aquifer celebrated between the Argentine Republic, the Federal Republic of Brazil, Paraguay Republic and the Eastern Republic of Uruguay.

141. Due to its increasingly strategic role, ground water is used in all Argentine socio-economic sectors ranging from small wells dug for a family's household needs in the suburbs of Buenos Aires, to more than 110 irrigation wells in the province of San Juan, Tullum Valley.

142. Regarding the legal condition of these waters the Argentine Civil Code establishes public ownership of surface and ground water in Article 2340, and the principle of 'special concession' for water uses in Articles 2341, 2342 and 2642.

143. Recently, in the case *Cariló* the Court of Appeals of Mar del Plata (province of Buenos Aires) set the appeal filed against applying the precautionary principle and ruled that:

> [a]s a previous and unavoidable step to the exploration and exploitation of an underground water resource, it is necessary to have the expressed authorization of the provincial Water Authority to conduct the drilling, a consent that is connected in an undivided way to the presentation by the interested party of a hydrogeology survey of previous technical validation, subject to the authorization of the provincial Administration which will confer the pertinent exploitation Certificate, whoever that may be.[94]

94. See *Fundación Cariló v. Municipalidad de Pinamar y Cooperativa de Luz y Agua de Pinamar s Amparo.* Judgment of Appeal Court of Mar del Plata, passed on 9 Aug. 2011. On internet: www.eldial.com/eldialexpress/home_ea_nd.asp?Edicion=14/10/2011 (accessed 18 Nov. 2011).

§4. Marine Pollution

144. In 1891, restrictions were established by Law 2797, which banned the dumping of waste into rivers and lakes, as we have already mentioned in paragraph 127.

145. Mentioned was not the only national regulation aimed to protect the quality of public waters. There were rules for wreck removal activities, which may constitute an obstacle to sailing. Law 20094 of 1973 was amended in 2008, with extensive regulation in order to protect the environment from ships and wreck removal activities as we refer in §5 of this chapter.

146. Before that, we will briefly mention the international regime for marine pollution by ships. The international agreement that regulates the marine pollution by ships activities is the MARPOL 73/78, adopted by the International Maritime Organization (IMO). Said agreement regulates the cases of operational marine pollution[95] and also the cases of accidental marine pollution. Said agreement was adopted in 1973. It regulated the pollution produced by oils, chemical products, hazardous substances and wastes. Then, the Protocol of 1978 was added to the original agreement thus yielding a sole text titled MARPOL 73/78.

147. At present, MARPOL 73/78[96] comprises a series of rules that are prone to prevent and minimize the pollution by ships through six Appendices: (i) Rules for the prevention of pollution by oil, (ii) Rules for the control of polluting liquid substances by bulk, (iii) Prevention of sea-transported hazardous substances, (iv) Prevention of ships' dirty substances contamination, (v) Prevention of ships' waste (garbage) contamination and (vi) Prevention of air pollution produced by ships. They are all in force, even the Appendix VI that entered into force on 29 May 2005.

148. MARPOL 73/78 establishes the sole acceptance of Appendices I and II as obligatory for the Member States, leaving the other Appendices' enforcement to their free election. Argentina ratified this agreement through Law 24089 of 1992 and by doing so, it formulated the following disposition: provided the required facilities in Rule 10 Appendix IV and Rule/Appendix V are not set then, Argentina will not be able to pass said guarantees established by said norms. The first of mentioned rules makes reference to dirty water reception facilities with adequate capacity and the second rule refers to garbage reception facilities with adequate capacity. The enforcing authority of said agreement is the Argentine Coast Guard.

---

95. The *operational* pollution is that originated in the commercial use of the ship, that is, mainly in the passenger or cargo transport.

96. See the work titled El Convenio Marpol 73/78. Un Estudio Detallado. Alis Cantano. Ministerio de Medioambiente del Reino Unido. En internet: www.derechomaritimo.info/pagina/marpol.htm#II.%20PROTECCI%C3%93N%20JUR%C3%8DDICA%20DEL%20MEDIO%20MARINO (accessed 16 Apr. 2010).

§5. Environmental Aspects of Wreck Removal Activities

149. The Argentine navigation Law 20094 of 1973 was modified in 2008. Such amendment particularly considers the negative environmental impact that ships and aircrafts produce when they are shipwrecked remainders, or they represent a danger to navigation. The legal regime was broadened with environmental foundations as we have analysed in another work.[97]

150. This is so, provided new legally protected rights are included, which are the environment and the free runoff of waters apart from maritime and fluvial navigation, whose protection is maintained. Considerations of the need and scope of environmental preservation or the hindrance of the non-obstructed flow of waters will depend upon each particular case.

151. The maritime national authority (National Coast Guard) would have to base its decision through remedy act that, as every act alike, will be preceded by external and internal controls and supervisions established by the legal system.

152. It is relevant to make clear as well that the consequences for obstacles or dangers to navigation or environment in an specific way have also been considered, through the replacement of Article 22 of the navigation Law 20094 of 1973.[98]

153. When the ships, naval ships, aircrafts or their shipwrecked remainders belong to a person residing in a foreign country, the corresponding consulate should be duly notified.

154. For the new Article 22 of the navigation Law to be applicable, ships and aircrafts must represent 'an obstacle or imminent or potential insurmountable danger' for the environment preservation or 'an insurmountable hindrance' for the non-obstructed runoff of waters.[99]

---

97. Julio César Villano, *Remoción, Extracción, Traslado y Desguace de Buques, Aeronaves, Restos Náufragos y Construcciones Hundidas o Inactivas en Aguas Argentinas y en la Cuenca Matanza Riachuelo. Recientes Modificaciones a su Régimen Jurídico* (La Ley: Anales de Legislación Argentina. Tomo LXIX E, N° 28, 29 Oct. 2009). This essay had been presented in May 2008 before the Navigation Law Institute of the National Academy of Law and Science of Buenos Aires.
98. The original Art. 22 stated particular rules for cases exempted of consideration in Arts 17 and 18 of the navigation law 20094 of 1973.
99. The derogated Art. 22 of the navigation law stated: 'The following are not taken into consideration in the Articles 17 and 18: ships, naval ships an aircrafts or their shipwrecked remainders of national, foreign, unknown countries or of Argentine, foreign or unknown domain that may represent an insurmountable obstacle or danger for maritime or fluvial navigation, in such a way that its extraction, removal or demolition must be carried out immediately according to a well-founded resolution of the maritime authority. The competent state body must act ex officio to carry out surveys and works needed to carry out the extraction, removal or immediate demolition of the obstacle. The owner or his legal representatives must be financially in charge of this, provided they do not use the abandonment right. When the ships, naval ships, aircrafts or their shipwrecked remainders belong to a foreign country, the notice to the consulate must be done previously as stated in the last paragraph of Article 17'.

155. Likewise, it is clearly stated that the Argentine Coast Guard must proceed to conduct surveys and works needed for the extraction and operations according to the norm under analysis. In this regard, the Ordinance 2 of 1995 issued by the Argentine Coast Guard comes into force.

156. The amendment of 2008 states that in Articles 17, 17*bis* and 18 of the navigation Law 20094 of 1973 the following cases are included by its regulations: ships and aircrafts, shipwrecked remainders of foreign or unknown ownership which may represent an insurmountable obstacle or danger for maritime or fluvial navigation, or that may also represent an imminent or potential insurmountable danger for the environment preservation or a hindrance for the free runoff of waters.

157. In such cases, the Coast Guard must act ex officio and carry out the necessary surveys and works for the extraction, removal, transport to an authorized place, scrapping or immediate demolition of the obstacle or danger. The obstacle owner or his legal representative must be financially in charge of this, provided they do not exercise the abandonment right.

158. At this point, it is important to note the need for the provision of specific funds for such activities because whenever the moment comes, even though the legal norm states the obligation of acting ex officio, without the proper financial means, these mandatory rules cannot be observed.

159. Regarding the Matanza-Riachuelo Basin, before the enforcement of Law 26354 of 2008, there was no legal regime that could specifically be applied to that particular fluvial zone.[100]

160. Its existence comes from the creation of the Matanza-Riachuelo Basin Authority (ACUMAR) through Law 26168 of 2006. Said Authority is an inter-jurisdictional entity with jurisdiction, control and fostering powers of industrial, public services supply activities and any other environmentally detrimental activity in the water basin that make-up the two aforementioned rivers (according to what Article 5 of mentioned Law sets forth).

161. The second section of Law 26354 of 2008 states the 'Special Provisions for Matanza-Riachuelo Basin' with the following text: In every action in which the concepts mentioned in Articles 17 and 22 and those concordant to Law 20094 of 1973 have to be extracted, removed or transfer to authorized places, destroyed or scrapped, ships, naval ships, aircrafts of national or foreign countries, their shipwrecked remainders and objects or constructions of any nature that may be found in

100. The ACUMAR exercises jurisdiction in the geographic area of the basin made up of the Matanza and the Riachuelo rivers and legally acts in the competence of the Secretariat of Environment and Sustainable Development (SAyDS) which depends on the Chief Cabinet Minister. It is made up of eight members: the chairman (SAyDS representative), three representatives of the national Executive Power, two representatives of the province of Buenos Aires and two of the city of Buenos Aires.

the Matanza-Riachuelo Basin, then the basin Authority created by Law 26168 of 2006 (ACUMAR) should be able to intervene.

162. The ACUMAR is entitled to sign cooperation treaties with the Argentine Coast Guard so as to facilitate and contribute to fulfil its corresponding functions, within its framework, and without the detriment of third party's rights according to Law 20094 of 1973, will be able to manage whatever comes up from the resulting objects of the extraction, removal, transfer, destruction or scrapping, affecting the enforcement of the actions foreseen in the Comprehensive Plan of Environmental Restoration of the Matanza-Riachuelo Basin.

163. As it can be observed, this new system essentially implies two main legal consequences. First, the obligation for the ACUMAR to 'intervene' without specifying said intervention scope, and whether it has to be done with a prior, concomitant or subsequent character to the activities. Experience indicates that it is convenient to carry it out previously so as to avoid problems in their development. Second, it expressly empowers ACUMAR with the 'enjoyment of the [commercial benefits] produced' that may arise from the sale of goods under its jurisdiction with the possibility of affecting the actions foreseen in the Comprehensive Plan of Environmental Recovery for said Basin (same Article of Law 26354 of 2008).

As we can see, at this point, the regime differs because, if the goods are not in the Basin, it is the maritime authority that carries out the auction, but if they exist within the Basin, then the ACUMAR carries it out. It should have been desirable to establish that the Customs must intervene when the goods (ships/aircrafts) are of a non-Argentine nationality and are located within the Matanza-Riachuelo Basin. Moreover, it has intervened in recent cases of wreck removal.

164. Finally and specifically related to the problems of noise pollution in the oceans, we would like to point out that Argentina has not passed legal norms or specific projects related to it.

More than a decade ago, Dotinga and Elferink wrote an excellent paper highlighting the environmental concerns related to this interesting topic.[101]

101. Harm M. Dotinga & Alex G. Oude Elferink, *Acoustic Pollution in the Oceans: The Search for Legal Standards* 31:151–182 (Netherlands Institute for the Law of the Sea. Utrecht University in Ocean Development & International Law. Taylor & Francis, 2000).

Chapter 4. Waste

§1. Introduction

I. Legal Framework

165. The national legal framework for waste includes the Hazardous Waste Act 24051 of 1992 and the Industrial Waste Comprehensive Management Act 25612 of 2002. Both are based on the imperative of responsibility from cradle to grave. However, there are remarkable differences between these two laws: as regards their scope, the Hazardous Waste Act is applicable in provinces subscribing to that system, while the Industrial Waste Comprehensive Management Act is applicable to countrywide waste generated by industrial or service activities. Article 5 of the Industrial Waste Comprehensive Management Act does not include pathogenic, radioactive, and household waste as well as waste generated by ships and aircrafts during ordinary operations.

II. Jurisdiction and Main Features of Waste Policy

166. The SAyDS has jurisdiction to regulate the main aspects on industrial waste and it agrees the minimum protection standards with the provinces within the Federal Environmental Council (COFEMA).

However, the provincial environmental authorities and the environmental authority for the city of Buenos Aires are in charge of controlling waste management in each of their pertinent fields through the identification of waste generators, and also to classify waste into three risk categories: low, medium and high.

§2. Objectives of Waste Policy

167. The main purposes of the Industrial Waste Comprehensive Management Law 25612 of 2002 are to:[102] (a) ensure the conservation of the environment, the natural resources, the population's lifestyle, the biodiversity and the ecosystems stability; (b) mitigate potential waste risks during its comprehensive management; (c) reduce the amount of generated waste; (d) encourage the use and transfer of adequate clean technologies for environmental preservation and sustainable development and (e) encourage the discontinuance of environmentally risky dumping.

I. Household Waste

168. The legal framework for household waste includes Law 25916 of 2004 on minimum environmental protection standards to manage household, municipal,

102. Article 4 of Law 25612 of 2002.

commercial, pathogenic, sanitary, industrial or institutional waste. Said Act was enacted by Decree 1158 of 2004. According to this law, household waste is any element, object, or substance that is discarded and/or abandoned after its consumption or use by people.[103] This law is not applicable to waste regulated by specific provisions.

169. Particularly regarding hardware waste from computers, monitors and other devices, In practice, those authorized companies take computing devices such as screens, printers and CPUs to destroy them with hydraulic guillotines and pneumatic screwdrivers. Those materials resulting from the destruction are taken to an area of classification; also plastic and cardboard are piled to send them to paper recycling plants later or eventually to the Ecological Coordination Metropolitan Area (CEAMSE).

The printed circuit boards are treated as dangerous waste and exported to start recycling. Cables are sent to a processing plant where conductive metals are separated. As a result of this, there is chopped copper (which is transported to copper smelting) and plastic (which is sent to recycling plants or rather to CEAMSE for its final disposal). Aluminium is regularly sent to smelting plants so that it can be used in doors and windows' manufacturing later. Iron scrap is then classified, pressed and sent to steelworks for its recycling with a smelting process. Regarding printers, print cartridges and toners cartridges are sent to an operator authorized to treat and dispose them. Concerning screens, the part containing copper is processed to isolate that material from the plastic. Copper is then stored and sent to smelting plants to recycle it resulting in plates, bars and other semi-elaborated copper products. Due to the lack of specific technology for pollution and glass recovery, cathode ray tubes are temporary stored so that an authorized operator of special waste can take it for its later treatment and final disposal.

170. The national authority enforcing this law is the SAyDS. The local authorities basically aim at setting up waste management systems for waste generated in their jurisdiction to prevent and mitigate potential negative impacts on the environment. Within this scheme, the COFEMA acts as a cross-jurisdictional coordination public entity.

171. The Hazardous Waste Law sets forth the offences and punishments that, regardless of other applicable civil and criminal law provisions,[104] range from a warning and a fine of up to two hundred national public administration minimum salaries to one year suspension of activities and the most serious one, the closure of the facilities where the offence was committed.

172. Recently, within the framework of the cooperation agreements entered into, the SAyDS adopted a pattern to calculate municipal solid waste comprehensive management costs.[105]

---

103. Article 2 of Law 24051 of 1992.
104. Article 26 of Law 24051 of 1992.
105. See www.ambiente.gob.ar/observatoriorsu/grupo.asp?Grupo=8076&Subgrupo=9560 (accessed 14 Oct. 2011).

II. Hazardous Waste

173. Hazardous waste is governed by national Law 24051 of 1992, as regulated by Decree 831 of 1992 and other supplementary provisions. The enforcing authority is the SAyDS.

Article 1 thereof, despite its poor drafting, determines the scope of the law and states that hazardous waste generation, management, transport, treatment and final disposal shall be governed by this Act when such waste is generated or located under national jurisdiction. However, the Law is applicable to waste that, although located in a province, has to be taken out of it; to waste that, at the enforcing authority's criterion, may affect people or the environment beyond the province's boundaries or when the applicable hygiene and safety standards have such economic impact that it is advisable to apply them across the country to ensure the companies' efficient powers to comply with those standards.

174. According to this law, waste that may directly or indirectly harm people or pollute the soil, the water, the air or the atmosphere are legally considered 'hazardous', especially waste mentioned in Annex I thereto, which lists the so-called Controlled Categories or waste having the properties listed in Appendix II of said law, which lists 'Hazardous Properties'.[106]

Household and radioactive wastes as well as those from ships' ordinary operations are not included in the law.

175. As it happens with industrial waste, this law requests hazardous waste generators, carriers and treatment or final disposal facility owners to register as such. In practice, the same national registry works for both types of waste.

176. A waste generator is any individual or artificial person who, as a result of any act, process or activity generates hazardous waste. Based on the amount and hazardousness of waste that they generate, they must pay a fee that shall not exceed 1% of the alleged activity's average yield.[107] Hazardous waste generators shall adopt measures to reduce the amount of hazardous waste they create, to correctly sort it out and do not mix it with other incompatible hazardous waste; to pack it, identify the waste containers and their content, enumerate and date them, as prescribed by the enforcing authority and deliver the hazardous waste that they do not treat in their own facilities to authorized carriers, specifying their final destination in the Hazardous Waste 'Carrier Manifest'.

177. It is forbidden to the hazardous waste carrier[108] to: mix hazardous waste with non-hazardous waste or substances, or with other incompatible hazardous

---

106. Appendix III of the Law lists the 'Disposal operations'.
107. Resolution 599 of 2001 sets forth the environmental fee parameters and expressly determines that it does not have '*a tax legal nature*'.
108. A corporation wishing to register as a hazardous waste carrier has to provide information regarding: (a) the company's owner data and legal domicile thereof; (b) type of waste to carry; (c) a list of vehicles and containers, as well as the equipment to be used upon any accidentally-caused risk;

waste, store hazardous waste for more than ten days; carry, transfer or deliver incorrectly packaged waste; accept waste whose receipt is not guaranteed by a treatment and/or final disposal facility and simultaneously carry incompatible hazardous waste in the same transportation vehicle.

178. The final step, that is, the environmental management, can be performed at treatment or final disposal facilities. Treatment plants are those facilities where hazardous waste physical properties, chemical composition or biological activity are changed to eliminate deleterious features, to recover energy and/or material resources or to obtain less hazardous waste, or where waste can be recovered or can be safely carried or finally disposed of.

Final disposal facilities are especially prepared places to permanently store hazardous waste under adequate environmental safety standards. Final disposal facilities shall include security landfills under the following conditions: (a) a soil permeability of no more than 10 cm/sec with at least 150 centimetres depth considering the landfill base as zero level; or a similar system as regards permeability speed or sealing; (b) a water table depth of at least 2 metres as from the security landfill base; (c) a distance from town as determined by the enforcing authority; and (d) a perimeter slip extension determined by the enforcing authority.[109]

179. In the hazardous waste regime, particularly regarding the watercourses, the Appendix I.b of Decree 831 of 1993 states a classification of the receptor bodies provided they could be final targets of said waste, once they were treated according to the compulsory treatment determined by law. Regarding water, mentioned decree provides a classification according to the present and future uses for superficial fresh water.[110]

III. Industrial Waste

180. Industrial waste is any solid, semi-solid, liquid, or gaseous element, substance or object arising from any industrial process, any service activity or directly or indirectly related to the activity, including potential emergencies or accidents, in relation to which its producer or generator cannot use it, dumps it or has the legal obligation to do so.[111]

(d) a practice test to provide the correct answer in case of an emergency arising from waste transport; (e) an insurance policy against damages, or sufficient guarantee set forth by the SAyDS.

109. Article 36 of Law 24051 of 1992.

110. It is the following: (1) Source of potable water with a conventional treatment. Protection of the aquatic life. Fishing. Aquiculture. Cattle feeding. Recreation with direct contact. (2) Potable water source with advance purification plants. General Irrigation. (3) Industrial water source. (4) Bodies subject to the mending and recovery of water quality. For brackish waters: Potable water source with advance treatment. Possible farming usage. Industrial usage. Recreation. Protection of aquatic life. For salty Waters: Potable water source with advance treatment. Recreation. Protection of aquatic life.

111. Article 2 of the Industrial Waste Comprehensive Management Law.

Recently, the Secretary of Environment and Sustainable Development, under the Cabinet of Ministries, set forth, through Resolution No. 522/14 dated 23 May 2014, summary proceedings for obtaining and renewing the necessary annual Environmental Certificate for the exportation of hazardous waste.

To obtain the annual Environmental Certificate, said rule determines that the registration or renewal of Hazardous Waste Generators under the Categories under control identified as Y10 (substances and waste containing PCB, PCT or PBB) and Y48 (materials or waste containing waste identified by Exhibit I of the Act on Hazardous Waste No. 24501) contaminated with Y10 and the approval of the Generator or Exporting operator to export said waste will involve a single administrative act.

The Resolution includes two Exhibits that list the documents necessary for the proceedings mentioned.

181. The criminal liabilities originally set forth by this law were rendered ineffective (vetoed) by Decree 1343 of 2002, which enacted such law.

Therefore, the industrial waste management criminal aspects are now governed by Law 24051 on hazardous waste.[112]

182. This Law states that the parties in the waste cycle have the duty to register with the pertinent environmental authority.

A. *The Use of Waste as Secondary Raw Materials*

183. Industrial waste importation and transport are expressly prohibited by Article 6 of the Industrial Waste Comprehensive Management Law 25612 of 2002. However, that same section renders said prohibition ineffective when it refers to waste entering the country to be used as industrial process supply.

184. However, there are exceptions. This law sets forth several requirements for exceptions to operate. First, the types of waste shall be included within a specific regulation. Second, said incorporation shall be made prior to the importation and third, the importer shall expressly show that such waste will be used as an industrial process supply. An industrial process is any activity, procedure, development or operation for the conservation, repair or transformation of raw materials or other materials essence, quality and amount to obtain a finished good through the use of industrial methods. This exception is also applicable to waste ‘in transit’ as stated in international agreements.

B. *Waste Management and Disposal*

185. There are three parties involved in the industrial waste environmental management: the waste generator, its carrier and the operator.

---

112. Article 60 of Law 25612 repealed Law 24051 on Hazardous Waste. However, said Art. 60 was vetoed by the national Executive Power through Decree 1343 of 2002.

186. The industrial waste generator has to take the measures necessary to: (a) reduce the amount of waste generated; for such purpose, the waste generator may adopt progressive industrial process technology advances programmes that give priority to waste reduction, reuse, recycling or appreciation, according to the regulation; (b) correctly sort out incompatible waste thus avoiding contact with each other during the management cycle; (c) package industrial waste when hygiene and environmental safety standards so require, identify waste containers and their content, date them and avoid mixing them, according to the regulation; (d) correctly treat and finally dispose of industrial waste generated by the waste generator's activity *in situ* to reduce or eliminate their hazardousness, harmfulness, or toxicity and if that is not possible, the waste generator shall proceed with that at duly authorized treatment or final disposal facilities that render service to third-parties, according to the regulation and the supplementary provisions and (e) reuse waste as raw material or input for other production procedures or recycle it.

187. The industrial waste carrier is only entitled to receive and carry waste accompanied by the authorized transportation document: the 'Transport Manifest'. The industrial waste carrier's main duty is to carry and only deliver waste in places authorized for waste storage, treatment or final disposal. If the waste carrier is unable to deliver the waste in the facility mentioned under the Manifest, he shall immediately report the situation to the waste generator and take the necessary steps to ensure the Industrial Waste Comprehensive Management Law 25612 of 2002 purposes are met. These purposes have been studied under §2 of this chapter.

Every waste carrier must take out a surety bond, a bank guarantee, be self-insured or have a similar guarantee to reinforce his pecuniary liability upon any environmental damage that he may cause.

188. The waste operator manages the industrial waste at a treatment or final disposal facility. According to this law, a treatment plant is a facility where the physical properties, chemical composition or biological activity of any type of industrial waste or service activity are changed to eliminate or reduce its deleterious, hazardous or toxic features, to recover energy and material resources or to obtain less risky waste, or where waste can be recovered or appreciated or where waste can be safely carried or finally disposed of according to adequate environmental hygiene and safety standards that do not significantly affect or put population's life at risk.

Final disposal facilities are especially built to permanently store industrial waste and carry out service activities that meet conditions ensuring the unchanging nature of the amount and quality of natural resources according to hygiene and safety standards that do not affect or put population's life at risk. Both types of facilities shall hold a registry of all operations performed. The facility owner is held accountable for environmental damage.

C. Urban Solid Waste in the CABA

189. On 24 November 2005 the Legislature of the city of Buenos Aires passed Law 1854 about all-embracing management of urban solid waste (the so-called law of MSW -Municipal Solid Waste- also called 'Law of Zero Garbage'). This rule was published on 4 January 2006 in the Official Bulletin of CABA (the BOCBA) and was established almost two years after it was passed by CABA Government Decree 639 of 2007. This is just one of many regulations which are part of the set of rules applicable to this important topic.

This law aims at guaranteeing previsions set forth by Article 4 of the national Law 25916 about home waste management, fostering the use of biodegradable materials, supporting environmental education programmes and the participation of cooperative associations and NGOs, regarding collection and recycling of waste. It also aims at reducing the generated waste and their dangerousness by establishing objective of gradual reduction and promoting an adequate and rational management of MSW. This rule sets the different stages and characteristics of the collection services and the requirements to be fulfilled by companies as well as the transference, treatment and final disposal of municipal solid waste.

As a main principle, the MSW management should be carried out 'without putting at risk human health and without using procedures or methods that may harm directly or indirectly the environment' and also fostering environmental awareness in accordance with Law 1687 CABA on environmental education (Article 4, Law 1854 CABA).

Pathologic waste is excluded from the enforcement of Law 1854 CABA, which are in fact ruled by Law 154 CABA. Dangerous waste is also excluded. They are ruled by national Law 24051. The industrial waste is ruled by National Law 25612 in accordance with Article 5 of Law 1854 CABA.

Law of Zero Garbage imposes various sanctions for those who leave MSW on the street after the established hours and for the failure to comply of those called *great generators* of MSW, carriers, and those responsible for centres of selection, treatment and final disposal. When the infringement is committed by a legal entity, those in charge of the direction, administration or management area will be jointly responsible with the represented company (Article 4, Law 1854 CABA), 'without prejudice to civil or criminal sanctions that may correspond' (Article 17, same law).

Taking into account the 1.5 million tons of waste generated by CABA in 2004 and sent to the different landfills of the State Society for the Ecological Coordination of the Metropolitan Area (in Spanish, *Coordinación Ecológica del Área Metropolitana Sociedad del Estado* CEAMSE [113] as the basis, Article 6 of Law 1854 CABA sets forth the following waste reductions: 30% for 2010, 50% for 2012 and 75% for 2017 forbidding the final disposal of materials that are 'both recyclable and usable' for 2020.

However, those goals have not been achieved, what caused one of the main environmental conflicts between the CABA and the province of Buenos Aires: the excess of MSW that CABA sends to that province. The underlying problem is that

113. CEAMSE is a public interjurisdictional company created in 1978 under the legal form of a state-owned partnership and made up of the Province of Buenos Aires and CABA in equal parts. Its area of influence is delimited by CABA and thirty-four town councils of the Province of Buenos Aires that surround CABA in the suburbs of the Province of Buenos Aires. That area has 8800 km^2 and a population of 13 million inhabitants. Source: www.ceamse.gov.ar (accessed 2 Jan. 2013).

landfills of the province of Buenos Aires –which receive waste from CABA and from various neighbouring town councils – are filled up and at full capacity.

Specifically, the Law of Zero Garbage authorizes CABA to deposit 750,000 tons of MSW annually. However, more than 2 million tons are sent every year.

That is why in January 2013, the CABA was analysing measures to reduce waste and implement technology that would allow the separation of the recycling material and bale it for its subsequent treatment and also put part of the waste in a stabilization process to use it then as landfill coverage.

IV. Special Waste

A. *Specific Regulations on Sustainable Use of Tyres*

190. It is widely known that an uncontrolled burning of tyres turn them into dangerous waste. Its burning releases decomposition products like greenhouse gases (GHG) that affect the ozone layer.

In May 2013, the National Environmental Authority passed Resolution SAyDS 523/13 (B.O. dated as of 17 May 2013) which contains definitions and guidelines for the environmental management of tyres with the development of a national strategy for the sustainable use of tyres in its life cycle particularly the waste tyres (Article 1). The guidelines that the environmental management of tyres should comply with are the following:

(a) *Reduction of Sources*: the generation of waste and elimination tyres should be reduced and minimized in relation with their quantity and their potential to cause substantial negative impacts and risks or environmental or human damage by using a proper design and innovation in the production processes, products and suitable systems of collection, treatment, valuation and final disposal.
(b) *Comprehensive Life Cycle*: tyres should be managed in such a way that risks, substantial negative effects, environmental and human damage are foreseen and minimized, even in all the activities performed during its life cycle (production, use, recycling, valuation, treatment and/or final disposal). This will be carried out by applying the best available technique (BAT) and the best environmental practices (BEP).
(c) *Proximity*: causes and sources of environmental problems will be considered a priority and dealt with in an integrated way, trying to avoid possible negative effects on the environment. This prevention will be organized into risks hierarchy (Article 3).

At the same time and in a rather generic way, the regulations establish that:

> the unauthorized abandonment and dumping of tyres, their open-sea burning and their disposal in landfills of entire tyres (excluding those used as a protection element in the landfill themselves) will be considered non-rational environmental actions and inappropriate management practices that are contrary to

and incompatible with the dispositions of the Law of National Environmental Policy 25675 (Article 5).

191. In the Buenos Aires province, 'special waste' is governed by the provincial Law 11720. Special waste regulations in the Buenos Aires province are similar to 'hazardous waste' ruled by national Law 24051 of 1992.[114]

§3. Import and Export of Waste

192. Please refer to §2 III A, in this chapter.

§4. Waste Taxes

193. An excellent study[115] published by the *Centro de Investigaciones Tributarias de la Facultad de Ciencias Económicas de la Universidad de Buenos Aires* (Tax Research Committee for the School of Economics, University of Buenos Aires) states that, in Argentina, there are no tax provisions including a 'green tax'; rather, there is a fossil fuel tax on fossil fuels, and financial incentives to encourage the development of new technology and clean energy sources.[116]

194. Local Law 3393 applies in the city of Buenos Aires since 2009. It levies the creation of municipal non-recyclable wet solid waste (particularly, biodegradable waste) when it exceeds the daily average of 1000 litres.

The Ministry for the Environment and Public Spaces in and for the CABA conducts a registry of the taxable persons. This tax is paid on a quarterly basis by means of the filing of a tax return.[117]

---

114. This provincial law can be read at the Buenos Aires province environmental authority, Provincial Agency for Sustainable Development (OPDS) whose website is: www.opds.gba.gov.ar/index.php/leyes/tema/5 (accessed 14 Oct. 2011).
115. Luis Omar Fernández (Dir) & Daniel G. Perez (Researcher), *La reforma fiscal verde y los tributos argentinos.* Particularly see s. 5.3. *Argentine situation*, which analyses the Argentine situation after a correct comparison is being made, based on R.H. Coase lessons in his work *The Problem of Social Cost.* It may be downloaded from: www.econ.uba.ar/www/servicios/Biblioteca/ bibliotecadigital/bd/cetri/reforma.pdf (accessed 14 Oct. 2011). The Coase Theorem is brilliantly explained by Robert Percival et al., in their *Environmental Regulation-Law, Science and Policy* 29 (5th ed., Aspen Publishers – A Wolters Kluwer Business 2006).
116. Regarding carbon taxes see Gilbert E. Metcalf & David Weisbach, '*The Design of a Carbon Tax*' 33 Harvard Envtl. L. Rev. (2009). The authors make clear, from the very beginning of the article that its scope is limited to the USA, but their conclusions are highly interested and clarifying for a comprehensive study of this subject.
117. This tax was specially criticized by companies from the gastronomic and hotel areas in Buenos Aires.

Chapter 5. Soil Pollution

§1. INTRODUCTION

195. Tyler Miller Jr. defines soil erosion as the:

> movement of soil components, especially surface litter and topsoil, from one place to another. The two main agents of erosion are flowing water and wind. Some soil erosion is natural – the long-term wearing down of mountains and building up of plains and deltas due to the combined action of physical, chemical and biological forces. In undisturbed vegetated ecosystems, the roots of plants help anchor the soil, and usually soil is not lost faster than it forms. However, farming, logging, construction, overgrazing by livestock, off-road vehicles, deliberate burning of vegetation, and other activities that destroy plant cover leave soil vulnerable to erosion.[118]

196. Just like Morrás explains,[119] it is estimated that 20% of the Argentine soil (about 60 million hectares) suffers from water[120] or wind erosion and soil salinity, particularly, in the Argentine areas of *Cuyo*, *Patagonia* and the *North-East* regions. These phenomena, jointly with global change, intensive farming and the extension of the agricultural frontiers and the expansion of urban areas have been damaging the argentine soil.[121]

197. Within this context, particular mention has to be made to the 'significant non-carcinogenic risks to Argentine inhabitants when consuming wheat grains affected by metallurgical or chemical factories', as it was found by a recent study conducted by researchers from the CONICET.[122]

---

118. George Tyler Miller Jr, *Living in the Environment: Principles, Connections and Solution* 552 (10th ed., Wadsworth Publishing Company 1998).
119. See the study carried out by Héctor J.M. Morrás, holder of a PhD from the University of Paris VII, France named *El suelo, la delgada piel del planeta (The soil, the planet's thin skin)*. INTA Technical documents. INTA Castelar, vol. 18, no. 103, February–March 2008. The author explains the argentine soil's properties with a detailed soil taxonomy map according to the *Soil Taxonomy* classification into six levels and twelve orders. This document can be found at the Instituto Nacional de Tecnología Agropecuaria, INTA web site: www.inta.gov.ar/suelos/info/El_suelo_ delgada_ piel.pdf (accessed 19 Oct. 2011).
120. Water erosion is a three-stage process, to wit: material preparation (detachment and removal), transport and sedimentation. Through this process, the soil and its particles are separated by water. This definition has been given by Roberto O. Michelena. *Water erosion*. INTA Technical documents. Available at www.inta.gov.ar/suelos/info/Erosion_h%C3%ADdrica.pdf (accessed 19 Oct. 2011). Furthermore, Morrás points out that water erosion specially affects humid climate regions with intensive farming. Among INTA's Technical Documents, it is worth mentioning the soil and environment maps for the argentine provinces and Islas Malvinas, which are available on the following official web site of the INTA: www.inta.gov.ar/suelos/info/documentos/informes/ indice_informes.htm (accessed 19 Oct. 2011).
121. *Ibid.*
122. Gonzalo M.A. Bermudez et al., '*Heavy Metal and Trace Element Concentrations in Wheat Grain: Assessment of Potential Non-carcinogenic Health Hazards through Their Consumption*' 193 J. Hazardous Materials 264–271. The authors found that 'Heavy metal and trace element concentrations

§2. LEGAL FRAMEWORK

198. The applicable legal framework for soil protection in Argentina is comprised by Law 22428 of 1981 and Decree 681 of 1981. The latter is supplemented by the adoption, through Law 24701 of 1996, of the United Nations Convention to Combat Desertification in Countries Seriously Affected by Drought, Especially in Africa, as adopted in Paris in 1994.

199. Law 22428 of 1981 creates the National Soil Regulatory Commission and also regulates the conservation and recovery of the Argentine land's capability stating that said activities are of private and public interest. It is a promotional law, setting forth that every area where conservation or recovery programmes are deemed necessary or convenient shall be considered Soil Conservation Districts, according to technical standards[123] whenever there are techniques with proven adaptation and efficiency for that or similar regions. This statement may be made by each government on its own initiative or upon request of interested parties. However, there are maximum limits to establish Soil Conservation Districts.[124] Decree 681 of 1981 regulates this law and enables the national government to grant subsidies. This means that the provinces may determine additional requirements if provincial subsidies are to be granted.

---

were examined in wheat grains and straw to elucidate associations between air pollution sources and soil variables. The mean wheat grain concentrations of Cr, Cu, Fe, Mn and Zn surpassed the tolerance limits stated in the international legislation for wheat grain and foodstuffs. When topsoil Ba, Co, Cr and Zn concentrations were higher than the legislation thresholds for agricultural and residential soils, wheat grain concentrations were also increased. In addition, Cr, Cu, Mn, Ni, Pb, and Zn revealed an immobilization effect of a cement plant and the atmospheric deposition input, with Cd in wheat grains being associated with a cement plant and industrial waste incinerator. The health risks arising from wheat grain consumption indicated that the inhabitants of Argentina are experiencing significant non-carcinogenic risks (Hazard Index = 3.311), especially when consuming wheat grains affected by metallurgical or chemical factories, as well as by air transportation from big cities.' Abstract accessible online through the following link from *Science Direct* Elsevier: www.sciencedirect.com/science/article/pii/S0304389411009393 (accessed 19 Oct. 2011).

123. Said *minimum* technical standards are determined by Decree 681 of 1981 and are the following three: (a) the current or potential soil degradation shall have an anthropogenic nature; shall be serious, and shall clearly affect farming. Any area with original natural soil permanently having a high degree of soluble salt, sodium, and toxic elements for ordinary plants or domestic animals, with low natural chemical fertility, with a high or suspended water table remarkably reducing or preventing the growth of roots in useful plants, requiring permanent or supplementary irrigation, that has suffered from clear cutting or deforestation or where any activity allowing the farming of our land is carried out shall not be deemed degraded land; (b) the chosen area shall be relatively homogeneous from an ecological and economic point of view to such a degree that enables the successful general application of techniques to be suggested; said homogeneity shall be based on sufficient basic technical information; (c) there shall be proven specific technical practices in the area or under similar ecological conditions that efficiently solve the current or potential identified degradation. The techniques that are considered proven for each district area, at the enforcing authority's discretion, shall be wholly explained by it with their specifications and alternative solutions, if applicable.

124. The maximum surface areas to be selected as Soil Conservation Districts shall include: (a) in dry land with an annual average precipitation of 700 mm or more, 200,000 hectares; with an annual average precipitation between 450 and 699 mm, 600,000 hectares, with less than 499 mm, 2 million hectares; (b) in irrigated land, 10,000 hectares. Art. 2, subs. d) of Decree 681 of 1981.

200. Several conservation consortia can be created within the Soil Conservation Districts. They will be the beneficiaries of the subsidies granted under this Law. Landowners, tenants, share farmers, beneficial owners and holders of title to rural property shall be entitled, under Article 7 of this law, to be members of said soil conservation consortiums. They shall mainly have two duties, namely: the duty not to use or manage land that may contribute or cause a remarkable reduction in the District's land capability and the duty to develop the activities that are paramount for the conservation of the land's capability.

201. The benefits for farmers participating in conservation consortiums are basically three: (a) the right to participate in stimulus granted by provinces to foster soil conservation or recovery, in furtherance of Article 5, subsections f) and g) of this Law; (b) the right to promotion credits granted by the Bank of the Argentine Nation to finance investments without national or provincial subsidies; and (c) the right to receive subsidies in furtherance of the abovementioned plans. Furthermore, the investments made under this law are exempted from the corporate tax set forth under Law 21287 of 1976.

202. As regards subsidies, the Secretary of Agriculture, Livestock, Fisheries and Foodstuff determines the costs of works to be carried out in each Conservation District, according to the plans submitted by the interested parties. Subsidies are not levied by any national tax, especially income tax. The abovementioned Secretary is also in charge of determining the amount of the subsidy and may receive technical advice from the National Institute of Agricultural Technology (INTA as per its acronym in Spanish). The subsidy percentage may range from 30% to 70% and even represent 100% of the investments expected in the plan to be developed in safe Conservation Districts located on the south of Colorado River. If the subsidy beneficiary makes investments in third-parties' property, the administrative Act granting the subsidy shall be recorded with the pertinent Real Property Registry. The grant of a subsidy may be cancelled when the works determined therein have been destroyed as a result of climate changes or earth movements that, at the authority's discretion, may be considered force majeure events or events of public security or national defence interest.

203. If the subsidy beneficiary fails to comply with its duties, this law states, regardless of any applicable criminal action, that the subsidies shall be reimbursed (updated and bearing compensatory interest that shall not exceed the annual 6%) if six months have passed and no certificate evidencing the investments made has been filed, or if the certificate has been falsified or the subsidized work has been voluntarily destroyed without the enforcing authority's consent.

204. Said punishment shall not be required if no investment was made or if the investment has been partially made due to force majeure that, at the Secretary of Agriculture, Livestock, Fisheries and Foodstuff discretion, may justify the delay due to its seriousness. In such case, a term of one year may be granted to complete the work undone.

205. If title is transferred or the rural property is leased, the obligation to reimburse the subsidy shall be, by operation of law, transferred *ope legis* to the purchaser or tenant.

206. This law determines joint and several liabilities for the professionals who have falsified or concealed the truth of the events upon filing the Conservation Plans.[125] According to the seriousness of the act, the Secretary of Agriculture, Livestock, Fisheries and Foodstuff may disqualify the professionals from their office for a term of up to ten years.

§3. Environmental Management in Polluted Areas

207. Argentina does not have a national legal framework applicable to the environmental management of polluted soil. In general, the rule applying as reference for environmental media values is Law 24051 of 1992 on hazardous waste. There is another problem: the lack of a systematic survey of provincial legislation. There are also several sectorial rules, such as those issued by the Secretary of Energy.

208. The General Environmental Law 25675 of 2002 may be used as a basic guideline to pass minimum standards for the environmental management of polluted soil. Up-to-date, those standards have not been issued by mandatory rules.

I. SAyDS' Management Manual

209. To redress the lack of a legal framework regarding the environmental management of polluted soil, two national boards depending on the SAyDS, the National Agency for Environmental Control and the Prevention and Environmental Recovery Agency, in July 2007 prepared a methodological manual[126] to deal with the environmental management of polluted areas. These tasks were developed in the framework of the 'Polluted Areas Environmental Management Program' created by SAyDS Resolution 515 of 2006. Its general goal is to create a management tool that identifies, systematizes, classifies and assesses the land degradation resulting from pollution and that defines the strategy to prevent, control and recover polluted areas through the development of the necessary regulatory supporting framework, considered a joint and agreed plan between the provinces, the city of Buenos Aires and the national government, in accordance with the COFEMA. Some specific goals are to prepare a National Inventory of Potentially Polluted areas and a Priority List with Polluted Areas to recover. Appendix A of the manual includes a list of potentially

125. The requirements to be met by said Soil Conservation Plans are set forth in Art. 11 of Decree 681 of 1981. It is mandatory that the Plans be signed by a licensed agronomist.

126. Authors explain the need to unify the methods in a single document because the bias nature and number of methods, technical criteria and applicable rules have caused important conflict, as shown in the case CENCOSUD S.A. and the concession of premises belonging to former *Obras Sanitarias de la Nación* in Beccar, Buenos Aires province.

polluting activities and their pertinent level of danger. Appendix B includes seventeen models of records to survey potentially polluted areas. Appendix C is a guideline to assess site verification research costs. Finally, Appendix D, which is under process, prepares a bid conditions model to carry out a verification research of potentially polluted areas, a detailed research of polluted areas, and their recovery and monitoring.[127]

127. They are all included in the *Technical Guide* for the Recovery of Polluted Areas as prepared by SAyDS.

Chapter 6. Noise and Vibrations

§1. The Civil Code Provisions

210. There exist many different legal approaches that generate, as it is usually seen in the professional practice, damages produced by noise and vibrations.[128] From an exclusively environmental point of view, we will say that the fundamental normative rule at the national level – apart from the generic right to a healthy environment set by Article 41 of the NC – is in the Civil Code. In fact, Article 2618 of mentioned Code sets forth, under the title of restrictions and limits to the property rights, that nuisance caused by noise and vibrations – among other causes – by activities in neighbouring buildings should not exceed the 'normal tolerance' bearing in mind the conditions of the place and even though there exists administrative authorization for those. According to the circumstances, judges may establish damage compensation or the cessation of such nuisance. In applying this Article of the Civil Code, judges must consider the production's requirements and 'the regular respect to property rights'; likewise, in their sentences they have to consider the priority rights emerging from previous usage or activities in the neighbouring buildings. Summary proceedings are established by Article 2618 of the Civil Code for nuisance actions.

211. The complaint filed on disturbing noises is not subject to the statute of limitations. Conversely, compensation prescribes after two years if there has been a wrongful act, pursuant to Article 4037 of the Civil Code. If no wrongful act exists, the right to compensation prescribes in ten years.

212. It is governed by strict liability, that is to say, that its attributive factor neither depends on negligence nor on fraud but depends on the causal relationship between the harmful conduct and the damage suffered by the victim. Doctrine states that:

> the liability arising from excessive conduct is a sui generis responsibility of a particular and objective nature that does not depend on negligence or illegality. Argentine case law also considered that the liability set forth under Article 2618 of the Civil Code is strict. It has been claimed that Article 2618 of the Civil Code is applicable to different neighbourhood-related issues: smoke, gas, vibrations, cracks, luminosity, engines vibrations, and soot, among others that are inherent to the building and do not depend on the negligent acts of those who lead or work therein. They should represent excessive nuisance; in other

128. Miyara wrote an excellent paper showing how noise causes legal effects in labour conditions (ruled by the Working Hygiene and Security Law 19587 of 1972 and its regulatory Decree 351 of 1979), in the environmental field (according to Art. 2618 of the Civil Code) and also in 'the authorizations and regulations, that deal with the permission for different activities which involve noise generation such as transport or entertainment'. Federico Miyara, *Analisis de la Legislación sobre Ruido y Vibraciones*. On internet it may be (accessed at: www.fceia.unr.edu.ar/acustica/ biblio/legis.pdf (accessed 14 Oct. 2011).

words, nuisance exceeding *normal tolerance*. The liability is beyond any intentional or negligent conduct.[129]

213. The National Civil Court of Appeals sentenced in a case that 'no compensation for damages can be sustained in favour of the neighbours of a factory' – in this case, a weaving one– for alleged noises, smoke and smell attributed to the industrial activity performed, as plaintiffs knew that the industrial type of area already existed when they bought their property near the defendant's facility, and because mentioned purchase was made after the latter had started to operate. Article 2618 of the Civil Code further states that judges have to render their sentences with due respect to the ordinary use of property and taking into account the 'priority of use' principle.[130]

214. In a typical cause of original jurisdiction, the CSJN recently passed a judgment determining a foreign embassy responsibility for noises and vibrations produced by an air conditioning device to a neighbour property.[131]

§2. Contraventional Code of the Buenos Aires City

215. In the city of Buenos Aires besides the national Civil Code, the local Misdemeanour (or Contraventional) Code of said city also applies. Article 82 of the Contraventional Code contains particular provisions and a special regime on bothering noises.[132] Likewise, it is worth noting that in 2004 a special law regarding acoustic contamination control comprising noises and vibrations was passed: Law 1540. Such local norm is regulated by Decree 740 of 2007 by the Chief of

129. Marcelo J. López Mesa, *De nuevo sobre el exceso en la normal tolerancia entre vecinos como factor de atribución de responsabilidad civil (El Art. 2618 Código Civil y sus posibilidades y limitaciones)*. Available on www.eldial.com.ar on 14 Nov. 2011 (accessed 17 Nov. 2011).

130. The court also stated that 'the experts evidence is particularly important in trials where the environmental impact of a factory under operation has to be demonstrated as the judge is able, through technical reports and objective data submitted by experts to determine the best criterion under Article 2618 of the Civil Code, to sustain the complaint if all the requirements therefore have been met'. National Civil Court of Appeals, Room E, 21.05.04. Case published under Judicial Doctrine 2004–02, 1204. Quoted by Santos Cifuentes (dir), *Código Civil Comentado y Anotado,* second updated and extended edition (Buenos Aires: La Ley 2008), 4:649.

131. In this case the Supreme Court highlighted that 'if both parties made verifications regarding sound pressure levels and they coincided that the sound produced by air conditioning exceeded the allowed levels municipal bylaw, then it is correct to approve the lawsuit – demanding the replacement of the air conditioning or reduction of such – due to that fact that the unpleasant noises exceed the normal tolerance that the complaining party is obliged to bear as a consequence of vicinity relations. If, according to ample powers given by Art. 2618 of Civil Code to judges, the cessation of unpleasant noises was established, then there is no point in demanding the compensation'. *Piaggi v. Embajada de la República de Irán.* CSJN 02.10.98. Sentence published by www.eldial.com.ar (accessed 12 Oct. 2011).

132. According to Art. 2 of said code, its norms are applied to the contraventions in the territory of the city of Buenos Aires or which have effects on it. About unpleasant noises Art. 82 establishes: 'That a person who disturbs the rest or public quietness with unpleasant noises which due to its volume, repetition or persistence exceed normal tolerance, will be punished with one to five days of public utility work or a fine of two hundred to one thousand pesos. When this action is carried out on behalf, to the protection, to the benefit of, or with the authorization of a person of ideal existence

Government of the City of Buenos Aires (formerly, the so-called City Major). The main criterion to determine responsibility for which accounts as 'unpleasant' or 'bothering' coincides with that of the Civil Code and it is the one that exceeds 'normal tolerance'. Said rule shall be considered according to objective criteria, in accordance to results showing titles that measure the noises and the intensity of vibrations.[133] However, the contraventional regime differs from the Civil Code, among other things, because the former establishes sanctions as fines and five-day public utility work and also because it considers altered behaviour when nuisance is caused by the name, in benefit of or with the authorization of a legal entity. Those are particular situations not established by the Civil Code.

216. Another difference lies in the norms applicable to the proceeding and the competent court. According to Article 88 of the Contraventional Code of the city of Buenos Aires, in case of responsibility, the trial is held at the local jurisdiction before the Contraventional, Misdemeanour, Contentious, Administrative and Tax Court if the local state is sued, and Law 12 of 1998 on Contraventional Procedures is applied. However, if responsibility is sought according to Article 2618 of the Civil Code, said action is ruled by the National Code of Civil and Commercial Procedure and the competent judge is the national civil justice.[134]

217. If action is brought in court against an individual before the Contraventional and Misdemeanour Court of the city of Buenos Aires, the complaint can be made before the prosecuting attorney's office of such jurisdiction or through a police formal complaint. When the unpleasant noises come from public transport, the compliant can also be filed before the *Comisión Nacional de Regulación del Transporte*, National Transport Regulation Commission. (CNRT as per its acronym in Spanish).[135]

§3. Noise Pollution at the CABA

218. The city of Buenos Aires is one of the noisiest cities in the world after Tokyo, Nagasaki and New York (La Nación newspaper 02 January 2012, p 12). Due

---

or the holder of a certain exploitation or activity, all these shall be punished with a fine of six hundred to ten thousand pesos. The rehearsal or playing of music in non-resting hours is not a contravention, only when muffling devices are used for sounds, instruments or equipment, when necessary.'

133. At that moment, the Decree 3902 of 1983 established a limit of sixty decibels for noises in commercial zones and an acceleration of 0,10/ms2 vibrations. Currently, Law 1540 of 2004 regulates both noise and vibrations in the city of Buenos Aires. At the same time, it divides it into various zones and establishes the limits of *'noise emissions'* and *'noise immissions'* allowed. In general, they are 55 dB during the day and 45 dB during the night.
134. On 2 Oct. 2003 the National contentious administrative and tax Court of Appeal passed judgment on the case *Barragán v. Autopistas Urbanas SA (AUSA) y otro* sustaining the statutory protection imposed by the neighbour of the highway 25 de Mayo of the city of Buenos Aires, imposed due to noise pollution and sentenced the city of Buenos Aires government and AUSA to carry out environmental impact surveys and an adaptation plan that may lead towards the reduction of noise both in the neighbouring public space and in neighbouring buildings.
135. The CNRT also receives serious complains about pollutant gases coming from public transport.

to this fact, it is necessary to implement noise maps –as graphics, numbers in charts or numerical data in electronic format- in accordance with Article 23 of Law 1540 of 2004 which regulates acoustic pollution in CABA. Said rule was modified by Law No. 3103 CABA of 2009.

Article 46 of Law 1540 states the permissible maximum noise limits and also values of vibration transmissions in outside areas, depending on the five areas into which the city is divided for those purposes: silence area, slightly noisy area tolerably noisy area, noisy area and particularly noisy area. Said Article also sets forth the permissible limits for inside areas and those limit values for noise emissions of movable sources.

Section VII of said law – regulated by Decree 740 of 2007 – has specific norms about the enforcing power exercised by the CABA government and also norms about sanctions that can be imposed. They range from a simple disciplinary measure to fines of ARS 1500 and also 'the seizure of elements causing pollutant emissions' (Article 42, Law 1540 CABA).

219. Specifically regarding the consequences of the environmental pollution in real state valuation in the CABA and more specifically the influence of the quality of air and level of noise on the pricing of real state, Mariana Conte Grand of the CEMA University wrote an interesting article called 'A first Approach to the Hedonist Valuation of Pollution in Buenos Aires'. Here, the author makes reference to a first approach to this kind of valuation for the area of Buenos Aires and points out that 'due to the lack of concrete information about noise and air pollution, the public transport is used as a proxy of it', using an estimate of maximum authenticity of a 'Linear Box–Cox function'[136].

I. Green Roofs

220. The Autonomous City of Buenos Aires has recently joined those cities fostering the implementation of sectors with vegetation in roofs in buildings and passed special rules promoting the so-called green roofs regulations. In these roofs, various species or even trees are planted with the purpose of contributing to environmental protection. Basic components are: a waterproofing membrane, root barriers, drainage and water retention layers and substratum of growth and vegetation.

Specialists make a distinction between two types of green roofs: 'extensive' and 'intensive' roofs. Extensive green roofs require a relatively scarce substratrum (5 to 15 cm) and support species that require little maintenance. Conversely, intensive green roofs can support trees and species that require a considerable amount of substratum and irrigation, and thus require greater maintenance than the extensive ones.

CABA Law 4428, which was approved on 10 December 2012 and published by the BOCBA on 21 January 2013, modified the Building Code of the CABA thus implementing particular regulation for green roofs in the City of Buenos Aires. These roofs are defined as 'the surface covered by vegetation that aims at

136. http://www.ucema.edu.ar/publicaciones/download/documentos/207.pdf.

contributing to the urban environment in a sustainable way' (Article 2 of said Law). This law also provides tax incentives – that amount to 20% of the Lighting, Sweeping and Cleaning tax – to homeowners who adopt this method for their roofs in accordance with some technical parameters established by a Weighting Coefficient (Article 6).

Chapter 7. Radiation

§1. Introduction

221. According to Tyler Miller Jr., '[i]onizing radiation, a form of electromagnetic radiation, has enough energy to damage body tissues. Examples are X rays, ultraviolet radiation from the sun and sun lamps, neutrons emitted by nuclear fission and nuclear fusion, and alpha, beta and gamma radiation emitted by radioactive isotopes', and continues explaining that '[i]onizing radiation can cause harm by penetrating a human cell, knocking loose (ionizing) one or more electrons from a cellular chemical, and thus altering molecules needed for normal cellular functioning' to conclude that exposure to ionizing radiation may cause damage cells in two ways: one is *genetic damage* from mutations in DNA molecules, and the other way is *somatic damage* to tissues, which causes harm during the victim's lifetime.[137]

222. In Argentina, there exist three nuclear plants that constitute the electric system in the country, to wit, Embalse Río Tercero, Atucha I and Atucha II providing the national interconnected system with 600 Mw, 335 Mw and 695 Mw, respectively. In 2011, Atucha II was set off and the construction of a new plant was launched: Atucha III. Likewise, The National Atomic Power Commission (CNEA as per its Spanish acronym) is working on the construction of a totally Argentine nuclear reactor: the Carem Project 25.[138]

223. Argentina is part of the main international treaties and agreements regarding nuclear matters.[139] In effect, the country has ratified the 1963 Vienna Agreement about civil responsibility regarding nuclear damages. The country has also ratified its Protocol and Supplementary Convention;[140] the Moscow Agreement in 1963 about the prohibition of nuclear weapons rehearsal in the atmosphere, outer space and submarine waters,[141] the London Agreement of 1968 regarding no-proliferation of weapons of mass destruction;[142] the Brussels Agreement of 1971 on civil responsibility of nuclear materials transport;[143] the 1971 London Agreement about the prohibition of the placement of weapons of mass destruction on the seafloor;[144] the London Agreement of 1972 on sea contamination prevention due to

137. George Tyler Miller Jr, *supra*, 266, 267.
138. Vis-à-vis this Project the CNEA publishes a series of new bulletins, which can be browsed on www.cnea.gov.ar/comunicacion/carem_hoy.php (accessed 24 Oct. 2011).
139. Particularly, see the regime on civil responsibility for nuclear damage according to the document titled *La Convención de Viena de 1997 sobre Responsabilidad Civil por Daños Nucleares y la Convención sobre Indemnización Suplementaria por Daños Nucleares de 1997*. A series of explanatory texts of the International Body of Energy. July 2004. On internet on www.iaea.org/ About/Policy/ GC/GC48/Documents/Spanish/gc48inf-5expltext_sp.pdf. (accesssed 24 Oct. 2011).
140. The 1963 Agreement on Civil Responsibility was passed by Law 17048 of 1966, and the Protocol and Supplementary Convention by Law 25313 of 2000.
141. By law 23340 of 1986.
142. By law 24448 of 1995.
143. By law 22455 of 1981.
144. By law 22507 of 1981.

waste dumping;[145] the 1980 Vienna Agreement regarding physical protection of nuclear waste;[146] the Vienna Agreement in 1986 on due notice of nuclear accidents and assistance in case of nuclear accident or radiology emergency;[147] the 1992 Mexican Agreement about the prohibition of nuclear weapons in Latin America and The Caribbean (the Treaty of Tlatelolco);[148] the 1994 Vienna Agreement on nuclear security;[149] the 1996 New York Agreement over total prohibition of nuclear rehearsal;[150] the 1997 Vienna Agreement regarding security on spent fuel and radioactive waste management;[151] the 1998 Vienna Agreement on Science and Technology promotion in Latin America and The Caribbean[152] and the 1999 Vienna Agreement on international surveillance plants for the total prohibition on nuclear tests.[153]

§2. Non-ionizing Radiations

224. Non-ionizing radiations are electromagnetic radiations which, as Berros explains,[154] do not carry enough energy and thus do not produce charged ions. Bonds between cell molecules are not broken. In terms of frequency, they can be distinguished into low frequency electromagnetic fields (such as power lines, household appliances and computers) and high frequency electromagnetic fields (such as radars, radio and TV installations, mobile phones and their baseline installation).

225. Following Berro's[155] paper, safety standards and the limits on power generation in Argentina are set forth in the Environmental Management Manual of the High Voltage Electric Transportation System as adopted through Resolution 77 of the Secretariat for Communications. In terms of radiofrequency, the rates of oscillation ranging between 100 KHz and 300 GHz are subject to a national standard set forth under Resolution 202 of 1995 of the Secretariat for Communications, Resolutions 3690 of 2004 issued by the National Communications Commission are also applicable. They state that the radiant systems should be adapted to the provisions set forth by Resolution 530 of 2000 issued by the Secretariat of Communications. As the author states in her work:

145. By law 21947 of 1979.
146. By law 23620 of 1988.
147. By law 23731 of 1989.
148. By law 24272 of 1993.
149. By law 24776 of 1997.
150. By law 25022 of 1998.
151. By law 25279 of 2000.
152. By law 25842 of 2004.
153. By law 25837 of 2004.
154. María Valeria Berros, 'Principio precautorio como herramienta de gestión del riesgo ambiental, su funcionamiento a propósito del caso de los campos electromagnéticos', in *Summa Ambiental*, ed. Néstor Cafferatta (dir) (Buenos Aires, Abeledo Perrot, 2011), 211 et seq. Under the footnote 4 of Berros' paper, mentioned author points out that the precautionary principle is related to a report issued by the World Health Organization named 'Setting up a dialog on electromagnetic field risks' published by the Public Health Department Radiation and Environmental Health, 2005.
155. Berros, *supra*.

the power to authorize and geographically locate power generators is vested in the local government, which is in charge of determining the necessary requirements to enable the generators' commissioning. Within this framework, the legal and technical EIA procedure is a requirement prior to installation.[156]

226. The precautionary principle has been used as a basis by the Federal Appellate Court in La Plata in the case filed by *Asociación Coordinadora de Usuarios, Consumidores y Contribuyentes v. ENRE-Edesur* in July 2003, to rule the complaint requesting the halting of an electric forced induction work involving Edesur SA and the Electricity Regulatory Agency (ENRE as per its acronym in Spanish) as defendants.

§3. Legal Framework: National Law on Nuclear Activities

227. This legal framework was approved by Law 24804 passed on 23 April 1997. It states that no individual shall elaborate, reduce, receive, acquire or use radioactive materials in any way, unless duly authorized.

228. Establishing nuclear policies and carrying out searches, controlling and supervising are functions of the national state. Such is the reason for the creation of The CNEA whose functions were reorganized thus creating the National Nuclear Regulatory Commission ENRN and the Nuclear Regulatory Agency (ARN, as per its acronym in Spanish). The company Nucleoeléctrica Argentina Sociedad Anónima was created through Decree 1540 in 1994 for generation activities, and 90% of its capital stock is owned by the national state.

229. The control functions of the CNEA that were then transferred to the ENRN are related to the following: application of isotope and ionized radiation procedures, nuclear policy description, the responsibility of radioactive waste management, determining the removal of nuclear power plants service and of any other radioactive plant, and establishing cooperation programmes with third countries, among others.[157]

230. The ARN's main functions are the regulation and supervision of nuclear activity regarding every nuclear and radiology security topic, the physical protection and supervision of nuclear material and the licensing and supervision of nuclear plants and international protection.[158] The ARN particularly grants, suspends and revokes construction licenses, and the setting, operation and removal of nuclear power plants. It also grants, suspends and revokes licenses and permits vis-à-vis the mining activity, uranium concentrations, search reactor security, pertinent accelerators including radioactive waste management plants and nuclear application to the industry and medicine fields.

156. *Supra*, 213.
157. Article 2 of Law 24804 of 1997.
158. Article 7 of Law 24804 of 1997.

231. To develop nuclear activities in Argentina a number of regulations passed by the ARN must be fulfilled, and licenses and permits for such activities must also be granted. The ARN grants licenses, which should have its proper authorization by the province where the nuclear facility will be located. Besides, every obligation regarding protection and non-proliferation must be met, specifically those signed by the Argentine Republic and also civil responsibility insurance for every nuclear plant has to be taken on. This civil responsibility rules are imposed by law 17048 of 1998, which ratified the 1963 Vienna Convention on Civil Responsibility for Nuclear Damage.[159] Its modifications set by the Supplementary Protocol and Convention were ratified by Law 25313 of 2000. The compensation for civil responsibility was set in United States Dollar (USD) 8 million by Argentine law for each nuclear accident in every nuclear plant. Hiring an insurance company is compulsory, and according to the law, the national state shall take on the remaining responsibility.

232. This law also states that in order to define the nuclear plant location, the CNEA will suggest a setting place. This should be approved by the ARN vis-à-vis radiology and nuclear security and by the provincial state law where the location was suggested. Such are the previous and essential requirement to start with this process.

§4. Management of Radioactive Waste

233. As Professor Ramírez highlights:

> in the environmental contamination arena, what is dangerous and spectacular is the sub-product of the nuclear activity in the first mineral extraction and preparation stages (leaching) as well as in the industrialization stages (uranium dioxide, etc) and especially that activity carried out in the nuclear plants.[160]

---

159. Article 9 of law 24804 of 1997 defines the concept of nuclear damage established by the Vienna Agreement. It states that the concept of nuclear damage comprises the following: body harm, material harm produced as a direct or indirect result of radioactive characteristics or of its combination with toxic, explosives or any dangerous features from nuclear fuels or of the radioactive products or waste in, incoming or outgoing the nuclear plant; also, material damage from ionized radiation emanating from any other radioactive spring inside the nuclear plant. This regulation also considers, within the responsibility of the owner of the plant, those damages affecting personnel and subcontractors due to nuclear accidents; those damages affecting the International Body of Energy's personnel, and damages brought about by nuclear substances outside the plant or the transport when at the moment of the nuclear accident it was reason for loss, robbery or abandonment.

160. Mariano Ramírez, *Contaminación ambiental en general e industrias. Conflictos y armonías.* Dr Ramírez (Emeritus Professor in mining and oil law in the aforementioned College) highlights that in the last Agreement signed between Mendoza and the Atomic National Energy Commission (CNEA) in 15 Oct. 1987, the eighth title (Art. 29/32) is included. Said title refers to National ecology protection and it states that the CNEA holds accountable for its own activities 'that should fully protect the environment' and should keep the Province informed of these; and if for example the CNEA abandons those plants that hold radioactive minerals shall first of all proceed to decontaminate according to OIEA and therefore will hold accountable for every possible damage that may be

234. In the 1994 reform, the NC introduced Article 41 whose fourth paragraph expressly bans the entry to the country with radioactive waste.

235. Law 25018 of 1998 defines as 'management' those activities needed to isolate radioactive waste in the biosphere exclusively derived from nuclear activity carried out in the Argentine territory. The necessary time for radioactivity to lower to such a level that can eventually enter the biosphere and its risks consequences for man and environment is also considered 'management'. The ARN sets the limits and procedures of such management.

236. Article 3 of said law defines as 'radioactive waste' those radioactive materials combined or not with non-radioactive materials which have been used in production or application processes for which no later usage in the same plant may be considered and those which cannot be disseminated in the environment due to its radiology characteristics and the limits set by the ARN.

237. The CNEA is in charge of the radioactive waste management. The generator of such waste is hold accountable for its safe conditioning and storing until it is delivered to the CNEA. At this moment, the generator accountability finishes. The moment when the transference occurs is determined by the CNEA. According to what is set forth by the second paragraph of Article 8 of Law 25018 of 1998, the operator of the generator plant cannot be disassociated regarding responsibility, at any moment and for any reason, before the radioactive transference to the CNEA has occurred.

caused to the Province' inhabitants as a consequence of its activities, according to the civil responsibility norms. Work presented in the Interdisciplinary Conference about Environment in the University of Mendoza (26–29 Sep. 2004).

Chapter 8. Other Sectors

§1. Noxious Substances: Pesticides, Agrochemical and POP

238. As Tyler Miller explains 'a pest is any species that competes with us for food, invades lawns and gardens, destroys wood in houses, spreads disease, or is simply a nuisance'. To control them men have developed a variety of pesticides (or biocides): chemicals to kill organisms we consider undesirable. Common types of pesticides include insecticides (insect-killers), herbicides (weed-killers), fungicides (fungus-killers), nematocides (roundworm killers), and rodenticides (rat-and-mouse killers).[161]

239. Legal regulations in Argentina regarding phytosanitary products, fertilizers, soil amendments and application equipment grant the National Service on Food Health and Quality (SENASA as per its acronym in Spanish) the responsibility of recording such products and those artificial or individual persons who produce their synthesis, formulation, division, trading, registration, enrolment, import and export and application on their on and on third-parties. The SENASA supervises products and companies jointly with the provincial governments without hampering the waste provisions that every county has on this particular topic.[162]

240. The applicator and product control, its tracking, waste and packing supervision generated shall be adapted to the Federal System of Supervision of Agrochemical and Biological Products' regulations on Resolution 500 of 2003 by the SENASA. The implementation of this Federal System of Supervision SENASA has total support of the INTA and numerous other transport and distribution unions and associations. This system comprises the producer's setup up to the final sale and its main purpose aims at supervising that the trading products are those registered in the SENASA, supervising its legitimacy, assuring the agrochemical tracking system and withdrawing those unregistered products from the market.

241. Particularly, the tracking of phytosanitary products is regulated by the Tracking System norms passed by Resolution 1230 of 2004 and which complements Resolution 500 of 2004, both regulated by SENASA.[163] It states the obligation of the holder of the Certificate of Use and Trading of Phytosanitary Products to have a special ledger where all transactions are registered.

---

161. George Tyler Miller Jr, *supra*, 618–621. The pesticides' names appear in bold in the original text of this book.
162. A good example may be the recent regulation passed in June 2010 by the county of Cañuelas in the province of Buenos Aires which apart from banning air fumigation in said county and the usage of herbicides within 2,000 metres surrounding urban residential or country houses areas and water, it also states that pesticides shall be applied within 200 metres around and after school time. Besides, it also lays out the duty of setting three line forest barriers surrounding rural schools.
163. Article 2 of this Resolution states that all the data that appears in the delivery note for every phytosanitary products shall contain: lot number of the product, commercial brand or number of registry of the product, volume corresponding to the lot number, capacity of the package of the lot

242. Regarding pesticides, Law 20418 of 1973 states tolerance and administrative limits of pesticides waste found in farming and livestock products and by-products defining tolerance criterion, zero tolerance and administrative limit. This regulation enables the enforcing authority to take some product samples at any place in Argentina. It is complemented by many other norms among which we can find resolution 934 of 2010 passed by SENASA establishing the requirements that shall be complied with by farming and livestock products and by-products for internal consumption. It also states a guideline for those prohibited products waste, establishes tolerance or maximum limits for pesticide waste, determines the chemical and biological phytosanitary products exempted from tolerance and limits, and sets the Prohibited and Restricted Active Principles.[164]

243. Likewise, the import, manufacture, formulation and use of Hexachlorocyclohexane and dieldrin products, whatever their commercial name is (usually called 'chloride') are expressly prohibited by Law 22289 of 1980.

244. The procedures and the scope of the registration of phytosanitary products are ruled by the Manual passed by Resolution 350 of 1999 issued by SENASA together with modifications by Resolution 371 of 2003 by SENASA. This norm states that those entities where these kinds of substances are produced shall be registered as well, whether these entities are located in Argentina or abroad and when the products are to be used in Argentina. Those entities where these products are produced on an experimental basis shall also be registered.

245. The fertilizers and soil amendments' import, export and trading are regulated by Law 20466 of 1973 on the supervision of fertilizers and soil amendments and its regulatory decree 4830 of 1973. For this case, SENASA is also the enforcing authority which in 2011 established the requirements for quality certification of those products registered in the National Registry of Vegetable Therapy and Fertilizers, Soil Amendments, Substratum, Conditioners, Protectors and Raw materials, through samples and lab analyses of such products for import and export.[165]

246. In the commitments with the international community, through Law 25278 of 2000 Argentina signed the Rotterdam Agreement on the consent procedure previously supported applicable to certain pesticides and hazardous chemical products that can be traded internationally. This agreement is applicable to prohibited or rigorously forbidden chemical products and extremely dangerous pesticides formulations. The fundamental objective of said agreement is to protect the human health

---

number and quantity of package according to the lot number. Should some of this information vary, there must be presented a new data registry in the delivery note.

164. This norm renders Resolution 507 of 2008 ineffectively. This norm from the Secretariat of Agriculture, Livestock, Fishery and Foodstuff partially substituted the previous Resolution 256 of 2003 of SENASA related to the maximum limits of pesticides in farming products and by-products, among other regulations.

165. This regulation establishes the model of certificate of samples, the control procedure in said tasks and the enforcing authority's power to order the prohibition of the sample goods when necessary.

and the environment in opposition to possible damage in the international trading of some dangerous chemical products, and facilitate the exchange of information on their characteristics and the import and export procedures between those states that take part.

247. The enforcing Authority is the SAyDS.

248. In this field of the Persistent Organic Contaminants (POCs), through Law 26011 of 2005 Argentina signed the Stockholm Agreement of 2000 regarding their reduction and elimination. The aim of this agreement is to include precaution before uncertainty, POCs reduction and elimination, developed countries financial commitments, and exhortation to the prevention of new POC chemical substances. The twelve United Nations Environment Programme POCs are: Aldrin, Chlordane, DDT, Dieldrin, Endrin, Heptachlor, Hexachlorobenzene, Mirex, Toxaphene, PCBs.

249. In May 2005, the first world conference of the countries signing the agreement was held in Uruguay, so as to agree on measures to reduce the impact on the environment. The agreement called on the states to set up a global action to treat pesticides, non-intentional industrial chemicals and by-products coming from combustion and waste burning opencast.

§2. Polychlorinated Biphenyls (PCBS)

250. As we have mentioned in paragraph 241, one of the persistent organic products (COPs) regulated by United Nations Stockholm Agreement of 2000 are the PCBs also called 'askarel'. They are fire-resistant, stable, non-electrically conductive, insoluble in water, insulating and non-inflammable chemical substances.[166] These characteristics make them useful for industry but very dangerous for the environment and the human beings' life. In Argentina they are used, among others, in medium and low voltage transformers.

251. Their normative regime is contemplated in Law 25670 of 2002, which states the minimum environmental standards for management and elimination of PCBs, and the Decree 853 of 1997, ruled by Law 25670 of 2002. Likewise, it is worth noting that for a specific case in the platform of the Buenos Aires Port some specific norms were passed in 2009: a Joint Resolution of the General Administration of Ports and the Secretariat of Agriculture, Livestock, Fisheries and Foodstuff. We will refer to all these below.

252. The regime created by law 25670 of 2002 has five[167] clear objectives, to wit: to supervise the operations associated with PCBs, eliminate all equipment containing said substances for 2010, to set the elimination of used PCBs, to ban its entry

166. More information available on www.pilardetodos.com.ar/nahuel/pcb/pcbd.htm. Visited 14 Aug. 2011.
167. Article 2 of Law 25670 of 2002.

to the country and to ban the PCBs production and trading. Article 3 of this law has many definitions, among which, we can highlight PCBs and equipment containing PCBs.[168,169]

253. According to this law 'PCBs' are: the PCBs (Biphenyls Polychlorinated), the polychrinated terphenyls (PCTs), the monomethyl-tetrachlorodiphenyl, the monomethyl-dichloro-diphenyl-methane, the monomethyl-dibromo-diphenyl methane and any other mixture whose total content of any of the aforementioned substances be higher than 0.005% in weight (50 ppm). At the same time, this law considers 'any equipment containing or that has contained PCBs (e.g., transformers, condensers, recipients with waste quantity) and that has not been decontaminated' as equipment containing PCBs.

254. The norm establishes a series of *juris tantum* presumptions, as: 'Those equipments of a certain kind that may contain PCBs, are considered as if they really had PCBs' unless the contrary can be proved. It is also a *juris tantum* presumption that 'PCBs, used PCBs and any other equipment containing PCBs are a hazardous thing in accordance with the last paragraph of Article 1113 of the Civil Code' which establishes an objective liability regime, as we explain in paragraph 412 and ff. of this work. It is also a *juris tantum* presumption that 'every damage caused by PCBs and used PCBs is equivalent to the one caused by hazardous waste' whose legal regime comes from law 24051 of 1992 and decree 831 of 1993.

255. Law 25670 of 2002 bans the production, the instalment of PCBs equipment, the import and entry to the country of PCBs and any PCBs equipment. Those containing PCBs for 2015 should have presented a programme for its decontamination or elimination before the SAyDS, since the norms states that for 2010 'no PCBs equipment can remain in the country'. If the possessor wishes to continue using them, then he must decontaminate them. The decontaminated equipment must be identified with a sign expressing so.

256. It is the PCBs possessor's duty to: identify the equipments and recipients of said substances and even the used PCBs with a sign indicating that they contain or contained said substances, implement an internal registry of activities related to PCBs and take the necessary steps to prevent risks to people and the environment.

257. This law creates the National Registry of PCBs Possessors, which is organized and functions in the SAyDS. The possessor of equipment having less than a

168. The correct interpretation of the last legal definition had decisive importance for a PCB's case solution in the Buenos Aires Port, as will be referred in para. 253 of this work.
169. Article 3 of said law also defines 'decontamination' and 'elimination'. Decontamination is the 'set of operations that allow those contaminated equipment, objects, materials or fluids with PCB's to be reused, recycled or eliminated in safe conditions and that could include substitution, understanding the latter as a PCB's substitution operation by adequate fluids that do not contain PCB's. Elimination means: 'those treatments and final disposition operations by means observed by the applicable norms on hazardous waste'.

litre of PCBs of total volume is excluded of registering. This does not exempt the enforcement of this law. The PCBs manufacturers and traders must also get registered.

258. The SAyDS is the enforcing authority of this regime and is obliged, among many things, to draft and present a national plan of PCBs management and elimination before the Federal Board of Environment (COFEMA as per its acronym in Spanish).

259. Sanctions may be imposed by the local authorities 'with previous summary proceedings that ensures the defence right'. Said sanctions consist of penalties, fines (which may be doubled if reiteration), disqualification and facility closure. These sanctions are applicable independently of the civil or criminal responsibility that an offender may infringe.

260. In a case occurred in 2008 at the Buenos Aires Port, the following matter was set forth. It had to do with the determination of who was the obliged person to register, when a port terminal had PCBs inside its port facilities that belong to the national state and when mentioned facility had been let to a corporation (the port terminal) through a concession contract.

The port terminal alleged that they were not the 'PCBs possessor' because they had received the PCBs from the national state and they had to give them back to the national state, at the end of the concession. They allegedly had a 'holder' or 'keeper' juridical status and because of that, they claimed to be exempted from registering in the National Registry because – they argued- the law only obliges 'possessors' to do so.

It was a literal interpretation of Law 25670 of 2002. At the same time, the author of this monograph professionally argued that according to the Argentine Law, it is never viable to be a 'possessor' of public domain goods. The quality of 'holder' or 'keeper' is always prevalent according to the Civil Code (i.e., there is always a relation of use and conservation of the thing, without the intention of acquiring the domain of it) since – by definition- the public domain goods are 'imprescriptible' and 'inalienable', among other characteristics. We intervened in that case and provided a non-semantic exegesis of law 25670 but a teleological one which could embrace the sense and aim of the norm and its coherence with the rest of the Argentine legal rules and the civil law basic principles and legal concepts.

Finally, the case was solved through a joint Resolution 53 of 2009 of the General Administration of Ports and Resolution 774 of 2009 of the Secretariat of Agriculture, Livestock, Fisheries and Foodstuff declaring that the concession company of the Buenos Aires port was the only passive subject of the emerging obligations of law 25670, and in particular that of registering before the National Registry of PCBs Possessors.

§3. Rational Use of Energy

261. Argentina signed up the United Nations Framework Convention on Climate Change of 1992 through Law 24295 in 1994 and the Kyoto Protocol of 1997 through Law 25438 of 2001. Article 2 section 1.a title (i) states that the Member States shall foster energetic efficiency in their respective economies as the most effective measure to achieve the carbon dioxide and other GHG emissions.

262. In accordance to the aforementioned, the rational and effective use of energy has been declared to be of national interest and priority, by Decree 140 of 2007, which created the National Programme for Efficient and Rational Use of Energy, which establishes certain measures to be developed in the short, medium and long-term. This would integrate the economic sectors mentioned in Appendix I (industry, commercial, services, transport and education sectors) and regarding the national and public sector, it grants the Chief of Cabinet the power to implement said programme in the National Executive Power's public buildings listed on Appendix II of said decree. The provinces, the city of Buenos Aires and local counties have been called to join this national programme in.

263. Particularly, Article 2 paragraph 10 of Appendix I of said decree highlights the need to evaluate the significant role of the Clean Development Mechanism (CDM) – in addition, the international carbon commerce – to support projects regarding energetic efficiency.

264. Resolution 825 of 2004 issued by the SAyDS[170] has approved the requirements for CDM projects, and the Argentine Fund for Carbon was created by Decree 1070 of 2005.[171]

265. To facilitate and foster the development of MDL projects in Argentina, the Argentine Carbon Fund, created through Decree 1070 of 2005,[172] has been created for the purpose of working under the provisions it sets forth.[173] Once the Fund's management is duly set up, it will depend on the SAyDS.

---

170. Said projects are presented to the SAyDS with a document containing the following information: project design in Spanish and seven copies, a copy in English and the project in digital format. Besides, it must also be presented a note containing its sustainable development contribution and documentation showing that the projects complies with legislation at a national, provincial and county levels applicable to the project in process. The proponent of said project shall be financially in charge of the costs of the technical evaluation of the project. Over a total of forty-eight projects presented in Argentina, only thirty-two were approved up to 26 Oct. 2011.
171. The SAyDS implemented a series of guidelines to identify and develop a MDL Project in the effluents management, energetic efficacy, waste management and forest areas which can be seen on www.ambiente.gov.ar/?idarticulo=5312 (accessed 26 Oct. 2011).
172. The SAyDS has implemented and published Guidelines to identify and develop the MDL Project in terms of effluent management, power efficiency, waste management and forests. These Guidelines are available at www.ambiente.gov.ar/?idarticulo=5312 (accessed 26 Oct. 2011).
173. As of October, 2011, the provisions were not passed; therefore, such rule has not become effective.

§4. Renewable or Non-conventional Energies

266. According to a special report drafted by the Energy Secretariat in 2004[174] and with the aim of diminishing the deleterious effects on environment produced by the GHG, Argentina:

> has the following options, in accordance to a survey by the Bariloche Foundation and published by the World Bank: an increase in the use of hydroelectric power is one of the most economical alternative to reduce emissions. In fact, it is expected that for 2015, more than 5700 megawatts of hydroelectric capacity will be installed. If such contribution could displace thermal generations, then in 2015, 18 megatons of carbon dioxide could then be replaced. However, large increases in the generating capacity may be difficult to implement due to social and environmental doubts related to mass hydroelectric developments.

267. Said report keeps highlighting that:

> the wind power is attractive and has a vast technical potential. The current [in the year 2004] capacity already installed is that of 26560 Kw. and an optimistic scenario of 3000 MW is forecasted for 2013. If this power could displace the thermal capacity, then that could reduce emissions in 1,110 megatons. Unfortunately, this energy potential happens to be limited by barriers to the access to transmission, a sporadic supply and high costs for those small companies. The wind and hydroelectric power together could reduce a total emission of about 8% towards 2015.[175]

I. Legal Regime of Wind and Solar Energy

268. In 1998, the Congress passed Law 25019, which states the national regime for wind and solar energy. Mentioned law was modified by Law 26190 of 2007. Law 25019 is ruled by Decree 1597 of 1999.[176]

269. Said regime declares the generation of electric wind and solar energy 'of national interest' in the whole territory and grants the National Energy Secretariat the nature of Enforcing Authority of said regime and its obligation to foster the researches of renewable energies.

---

174. *Descripción, Desarrollo y Perspectivas de las Energías Renovables en la Argentina y en el Mundo*. Report by The National Energy Secretariat, May 2004, 18: On Internet, available on: http://energia.mecon.ar/publicaciones/DescripcionDesarrolloyPerspectivas.pdf (accessed 22 Nov. 2011).
175. *Descripción, Desarrollo y Perspectivas de las Energías Renovables en la Argentina y en el Mundo, supra.*
176. This decree states, among other norms, the benefits, term and limitations for this regime.

270. It is the norm of incentives that imposes the obligation for the enterprises which generate these kinds of energies to have an address in Argentina and be incorporated under the country's regulations, particularly, according to the regulations of the Law 19550 of Commercial Companies. The beneficiaries of the tax postdating are only those individuals and corporations who have the condition of registered contributors in the Value Added Tax (VAT) with address in the country and who are holders of installations or projects of Installations of Solar or Wind Energy Generators Plants whose production is destined to Wholesale Electric Market (MEM as per its acronym in Spanish) and/or the provisions of public services.

271. Besides, the interested parties should present a Project of the Installations of a Solar and Wind Energy Generation Plant before the National Energy Secretariat. Said project must have an investment plan, the estimated date of the implementation of the equipment, the official and final installation and a list of goods, works and services with its amount and value related to the Project. The Energy Secretariat can establish the additional requirements through founded resolutions.

272. According to the tax postdating for capital investments, the due payments to the valued added tax (VAT, which is of 21%) can be postponed for fifteen years as of the enforcement of said law. The debts will subsequently be honoured in fifteen annual payments as of the last debt expiry date.[177]

273. Law 25019 of 1998 also sets forth that the Fiduciary Fund for Renewable Energies will be administered by the Federal Board of Electric Energy and that will be assigned to promotion aims.[178] It also establishes a tax stability guarantee for fifteen years.

274. Provinces have been invited by this national law to pass norms establishing tax exemptions for the generation of wind or solar electric energy.

177. Article 3 of Law 26190 of 2007.
178. The concrete benefits covered by Art. 5 of this law are: (1) Pay up to one point 5% per Kilowatt-hour (ARS 0.015 per kWh) effectively generated by wind systems installed or to be installed, which destine their energy to wholesale market or are destined to the supply of public services. (2) Pay up to zero point nine pesos per Kilowatt-hour (ARS 0.9 per kWh) to the user's convenience with photovoltaic generators by geothermal energy systems, biomass tidal power, dumping gases, depuration plants gases and biogas to be installed which destine their energy to wholesale market or are destined to the supply of public services. Those considered in law 26093 are exempted from this payment. (3) Pay up to one point 5 cents per Kilowatt-hour (ARS 0.015 per kWh) effectively generated by hydroelectric systems to be installed of up to thirty Mega Watts (30 MW) which destine their energy to the wholesale market or are destined to the supply of public services.

Part II. Nature Conservation and Management

Chapter 1. Monuments and Landscapes

§1. Natural Monuments

275. In Argentina, the Protected Areas (PA) Law 22351 of 1980 defines 'natural monuments' as the areas, objects, and living flora or fauna that are of aesthetic interest, have a historic or scientific value and are granted full protection. They are considered inviolable areas, thus no activity can be performed in relation thereto, except for official inspections or scientific research works that are permitted by the enforcing authority and are deemed necessary for their protection and care by visitors.[179]

276. Within the Argentine National Parks system, there currently are two natural monuments, to wit, the Petrified Forest National Monument in Santa Cruz province and the Laguna de los Pozuelos Biosphere Reserve in Jujuy province.

277. Furthermore, Law 24702 of 1996 declared the living North Andean Deer and similar species to be national natural monuments (according to Article 8 of the PA Law) and assigns the National Parks Administration the duty to create a species management plan in areas under its jurisdiction. The Patagonian right whale and the Jaguar have also been declared to be national natural monuments.

278. The provinces of Misiones, Corrientes and Entre Ríos have enacted laws which are similar to those enacted by the national government, and thus declared several native species of flora and fauna to be provincial natural monuments.

§2. Landscapes

279. In the international sphere, the legal concept of 'landscape' began to receive environmental protection in the early 1990s. In fact, the Convention concerning the Protection of the World Cultural and Natural Heritage of 1972 did not specifically include the protection for landscapes.

---

179. The concept of *environmental monument* was boosted by the Convention for the Protection of Flora, Fauna and Natural Scenic Beauties of America (Washington, 1940).

280. The Argentine Federal Law makes an indirect reference to landscapes under the PA Law 22351 of 1980, Decree 2148 of 1990, Decree 2149 of 1990 and Decree 453 of 1994. These regulations specifically ban 'any act or omission that may adversely affect the landscape or the biological balance of National Parks unless they involve strict defensive measures to ensure National Security, according to the purposes and policies in force regarding this matter'.[180]

180. Luis Castelli & Valeria Spallaso, *Planificación y Conservación del Paisaje. Herramientas para la Protección del Patrimonio Natural y Cultural (Landscape Planning and Conservation. Tools to protect the Natural and Cultural Heritage)* (Buenos Aires: Naturaleza para el Futuro Foundation, 2007, 128. Posted on the Internet at: www.naturalezaparaelfuturo.org/pdf/planificacion_ conservacion_paisaje.pdf (accessed 31 Oct. 2011).

Chapter 2. Parks and Reserves

§1. Legal Regime for the National System of Fire Management

281. With national Law 26815 from 2013 (published in the Official Gazzette on 16 January 2013) the Congress established a regime of minimum standards of environmental protection regarding forest and rural fires which can be applied in all the Argentine territory, and also the rules for the prevention, suppression and fighting of forest and rural fires that burn living or dead vegetation in native or implanted forests, protected natural areas, farming areas, grasslands, pastures, bushes and wetlands in those areas where 'building structures are intermingled with vegetation away from the strictly urban or structural area'. 'Planned fires that burn under pre-established environmental conditions and those fires aiming at handling territorial units' (Article 2) are also included in mentioned law.

In order to implement these regulations, the national system for fire management is established. It is made up by the National Service of Fire Management, other agencies determined by the provinces, the city of Buenos Aires and the Administration of National Parks. This National System has three general objectives: to protect the environment from fire damages, to look after people's security and the security of those in charge of fighting fire and to establish proper mechanisms for a good performance. It also has three specific objectives: to establish mechanisms for an efficient management of fire as a defence for the environment, to coordinate and technically and operationally assist agencies involved and foster people's awareness about the impacts deriving from the managing of fires. This national system is organized into regions.

The enforcement agency is the SAyDS and the competent Authorities are those established by each province or in the city of Buenos Aires jurisdiction.

Specifically, fire protection (Article 10) is organized under Plans for Fire Management that function in three different jurisdictions: local, regional and national. Besides, a national system of 'Early Alert' and 'Fire Risk Assessment' are established in order to anticipate those risks.

The Federal System for Fire Management created by this regime also establishes obligations of local jurisdictions (Article 13), obligations for the Fire Chief (Article 13) and other individuals (Articles 16–22).

Likewise, this regulation creates the National Fund for Fire Management to be managed by the National Enforcement Authority. This Fund has not been implemented yet.

This scenario is completed with a regime of infringements and sanctions. The following are infringements: to carry or light fires in forests and pastures infringing the law, failure to comply with the obligation to give notice to the closest authority to a fire, to light a fire or carry out burnings without being duly authorized, not having protection plans and hinder fire fighting personnel's work. Sanctions range from disciplinary measures to fines, the closure of institutions and the loss of concessions and tax and credit benefits that the offender may have. The procedure is ruled by the administrative procedure rules of the place where the infringement has been committed.

§2. The Physical Context

282. A report prepared in 2007 by the National Parks Administration (APN as per its acronym in Spanish) reveals that:

> in the first place, there is evidence of an express sharp division between the two most typical categories: national/provincial parks and the Protected Areas managed resources: the first category represents 16.86% of the total surface while the second category represents 76.14%. This polarization is also evident because, while category II is under national jurisdiction (the APN jurisdiction), category VI is mainly governed by provinces. Generally speaking, categories can be classified into totally or strictly protected categories (categories I-IV) and partially protected categories (categories V-VI) and the percentages are similar: 22.5% and 77.5% respectively. If this situation is compared to that 10 years ago (APN, 1998) it is evidenced that, despite growth, the percentages have remained practically the same.[181]

283. Between 1997 and 2006 there has been an important increase of PA in Argentina. During that period 153 new PA have been created, which means 5,981,000 hectares under such system. In total, there are 435 PA[182] representing 21.5 million hectares across the country.[183]

284. Despite biodiversity and the huge fishery resources at sea and at the Argentine continental shelf, the protected marine areas have not yet been defined. By 2012, 'at least 10% of the argentine marine area shall be a marine protected area, as it was agreed under the Convention on Biological Diversity'.[184]

285. The International Union for the Conservation of Nature (IUCN) declared the Earth and/or sea surface to be a protected area. The IUCN is in charge of the protection and maintenance of biodiversity, and associated natural and cultural resources as well as their management through legal means. In 1994, the IUCN

181. *Las Areas Protegidas en Argentina. Herramienta superior para la conservación de nuestro patrimonio natural y cultural (Protected Areas in Argentina: a tool to protect our natural and cultural heritage).* National Parks Administration in cooperation with Wild Life Foundation for Argentina. Buenos Aires, September 2007, 21.

182. As by the year 2006.

183. *Las Areas Protegidas de la Argentina. Herramienta superior para la conservación de nuestro patrimonio natural y cultural. (Protected Areas in Argentina: A tool to protect our natural and cultural Heritage).* National Parks Administration in cooperation with Wild Life Foundation in and for Argentina. Buenos Aires, September 2007, 14. This lengthy and complete document has been posted on the Internet at: www.parquesnacionales.gov.ar/docAP/DocAP.pdf (accessed 31 Oct. 2011).

184. Source: World Wildlife Foundation. Argentina points out that 'the current sea and coastline surface with some degree of protection represents a slightly 1%. From the 47 coastal and marine protected areas in our country, less than 15% are under management plans in force and more than 80% do not have sufficient resources to meet the basic conservation goals'. For more details, see the Foundation's web site at: www.vidasilvestre.org.ar/que_hacemos/nuestra_solucion/cuidar_nuestro_mundo_natural/ordenamiento_territorial/nuestro_mar/areas_marinas_protegidas/ (accessed 31 Oct. 2011).

World Commission on PA defined the criteria for the PA and set forth six Management Categories in descending order of protection.[185]

§3. The Federal Level

286. Since the 1994 national Constitutional reform, provinces have the original power on natural resources located within their territories. Therefore, each province is entitled to exercise jurisdiction on their PA. Most provinces have enacted laws on PA within their territories. These legal systems coexist with the Federal PA, that is, areas under national jurisdiction, as regulated by Law 22351 of 1980 whose enforcing authority is the National Parks Administration. As in other cases, COFEMA's coordination is paramount to make progress on this issue.

287. Law 22351 of 1980 defines three categories for National PA, to wit: Natural Park, Natural Monument and National Reserve. Each of them has specific rules for environmental management.

288. Through Decree 2148 of 1990, Decree 2149 of 1990 and Decree 453 of 1994, the environmental Management categories are expanded to include the 'Strict Nature Reserve' and the 'Wild Nature Reserve' at national level. Decree 453 of 1990 also determined the final limits on Strict Nature Reserves.

289. The National Strict Nature Reserve System is consistent with IUCN Category I. The determination of areas as National Strict Nature Reserves shall be made through Executive Order and they shall be deemed PA under national jurisdiction

185. The six categories are the following: Category I: Strict Natural Reserve. Primary Objective: comprehensive protection. They refer to areas where human visitation is strictly restricted to controlling staff or researchers. Category II: National (or Provincial) Park. Primary objective: the conservation of ecosystems and the support of tourism. The goal is to ensure no human settlement is located there (the Argentine legislation does not directly allow settlements). The presence of people is permitted for recreational-tourist, educational and compatible scientific purposes insofar as biodiversity be preserved. Category III: Natural Monument. Primary Objective: the conservation of natural features. The provisions are very similar to the Park's provisions. Category IV: Habitat/Species Management Area. Primary Objective: Active Management for conservation. There is environmental and/or population or community management for the species or community conservation in the area. Category V: Protected Landscape. Primary objective: Landscape conservation and recreation. Priority is given to the conservation of the landscape, the cultural and traditional heritage rather than to biodiversity. Category VI: Managed Resource Protected Area. Primary Objective: sustainable use of natural ecosystems. Small human settlements and productive activities based on the use of products of nature are allowed together with tourism. A slight conversion of the habitat is permitted for crops. See *Las Areas Protegidas en Argentina. Herramienta superior para la conservación de nuestro patrimonio natural y cultural. (Protected Areas in Argentina. A tool to protect our natural and cultural Heritage).* National Parks Administration in cooperation with Wild Life Foundation in and for Argentina. Buenos Aires, September 2007. Professor Adrian Phillips is the author and editor of the set of *Directrices sobre buenas prácticas en áreas protegidas (Instructions on protected areas good practices).* These Instructions are applicable to Category V areas, Protected Marine and Earth Settings as published in 2002 by the Cardiff School of City and Regional Planning and the IUCN. They are available at http://data.iucn.org/dbtw-wpd/edocs/PAG-009-Es.pdf (accessed 28 Oct. 2011).

with the maximum guarantees for the protection of the Argentine biodiversity. Areas with high biological value representing the different ecosystems across the country or having an important number of native flora and fauna species shall be considered National Strict Nature Reserves.[186]

290. The enforcing authority is the National Parks Administration, which acts in accordance with the PA National System Guidelines. As regards national strict nature reserves in Argentina, apart from the general prohibitions to carry out activities that may adversely affect the natural features or that may threaten to reduce biodiversity (except for the necessary flora and fauna control and management activities), there are specific prohibitions, such as: the extraction of natural resources or any other use of such resources, mineral exploration, fishing and hunting activities and any other type of wild fauna harassment or disturbance and the pick-up of flora (unless it is authorized for management or scientific purposes), the incorporation, transplant and spread of exotic flora and fauna; the incorporation of domestic animals, unless it is necessary for strict nature reserves management and control; the use of toxic substances (unless it is authorized for management or scientific purposes), human settlements, general public access, and the construction of buildings, except for the necessary minimum permissions for scientific observation, control and management.

186. Article 2 of Decree 2148 of 1990.

Chapter 3. Wildlife Protection

§1. Introduction

291. In regard to general wildlife protection, in Argentina there is an old regulation, Law 14346 of 1954, which is still in force and regulates wildlife protection.

Mentioned law sets forth that 'any person who mistreats animals or exercises animal abuse' shall be punished with fifteen days in jail. According to this law, mistreating animals and exercising animal abuse include: not feeding animals properly, punishing and harming them, giving them drugs for non-therapeutic purposes, operating on them without a license, abandoning the specimens used for experiments, running over them and thus causing them harm, torturing them, slaughtering animals with evil and organizing any private or public animal fight and bullfight where animals may be killed or hurt.

§2. Specific Legislation

292. In Argentina, and up to 1981, wildlife protection was specifically governed by Law 13908 of 1950, which basically prohibited hunting animals in territories under national and federal jurisdiction. In 1981, said law was replaced by Law 22421 and its regulatory Decree 691 of 1981 that are currently in force, together with many supplementary provisions.

293. Law 22421 of 1981 sets forth conservation principles, includes rules on the hunting, management and health of fauna, sets forth rules on inter-provincial and international trade and describes the national enforcing authority's powers. It also includes specific provisions on crimes, offences and punishments applicable to any person who infringes these rules. The species under its jurisdiction are described in the exhibits thereto. It also defines wild animals as 'free-living animals located in natural or artificial environments; wild animals under man's control, in captivity or semi captivity and originally domestic animals that, under any circumstance, return to wildlife becoming wild animals'. The species inter-provincial or international transport shall be governed by a 'Traffic Guide' issued by the pertinent authority to register that the animal was hunted in permitted areas with the consent of the premise's owner or administrator. Hunting animals without permission shall be punished with up to one year in jail.

The punishment may be raised to five years imprisonment if it involves a wild animal whose hunting or smuggling is either prohibited or forbidden. The same punishment shall apply to those who carry, store, purchase, sale or industrialize products or by-products resulting from poaching.

294. In 1982, Law 22344 came into force and adopted the CITES. Its enforcing authority is the SAyDS. This law is regulated by Decree 522 of 1997 that designates the Wildlife Committee as the administrative authority. The Committee's duties are: to grant, cancel, revoke, amend and withdraw CITES import and export certificates, certificates of introduction from the sea or re-export permits; to keep a record of traded specimens; to control the conditions for the transport, care and preparation for shipment of living specimens that are subject to trade; to confiscate or participate in the confiscation of specimens traded in violation of Law 22344 of 1982 and to return them to their country of origin to determine their permanent or temporary destination; to state the characteristics of the marking of specimens under international trade; to organize and keep an updated Record of Offenders; to suggest the amendment of Appendices I and II and submit the lists to add species under Appendix III of CITES; to designate the qualified customs offices for the entry and exit of specimens under international trade and prepare and submit annual reports according to CITES Convention.

295. The SAyDS must conduct proceedings according to Resolution 475 of 2005 in order to impose sanctions resulting from environmental violations. Resolution 475 of 2005 includes the summary proceedings to be followed for this purpose. It is supplemented by National Law 19549 on Administrative Procedures and the National Code of Commercial and Civil Procedure.[187]

296. Likewise, we should highlight that in Argentina there exits various wetlands that have been designates as *Ramsar* sites, due to their environmental importance.

297. We have mentioned in another work[188] that there exist certain differences between a *Ramsar* and a *Natura 2000* site.

First, a *Ramsar* site is a wetland of international importance especially as an aquatic bird's habitat and it is under the regulation of the Convention signed in *Ramsar* in 1971.[189] This convention holds the name of the Iraqi city in which it was

187. Summary proceedings are filed with the SAyDS Environmental Offences board, which verifies whether any proceeding prior to the preliminary hearing (Acknowledgement Record) is consistent with the guidelines set forth under Art. 5 of Resolution 475 of 2005. This regulation determines the participation of an Advisory Committee on Environmental Offences. Once the minute has been prepared, it shall be submitted to the Environmental Offences Director together with a technical environmental report and any evidence of the alleged offence. This Resolution also governs the filing of complaints, which can be oral complaints. In the event an environmental offence is confirmed, the accused shall have ten days for his deposition. The evidence having been submitted, and the deposition having been made, the investigating authority shall submit his justified report. This report shall be then submitted to the General Office on Legal Matters to control its legality and further filed with the Secretary of Environment and Sustainable Development for its signing and for the conclusion of the proceedings through the acquittal or punishment of the offender.

188. Julio César Villano, *Regímenes Jurídicos Aplicables a la Contaminación del Espejo de Agua Portuario: Casos de los Puertos de Buenos Aires (Argentina) y Nantes Saint-Nazaire (Francia)*, a thesis by the author of this work to obtain the degree of Master in Environmental Sciences granted by the University of Business and Social Sciences (UCES). The thesis was directed by Dr Hugo Caminos, Hon. Judge of the International Tribunal for the Law of the Sea (ITLOS). It has been completed and approved. Its oral defence will be carried out soon.

189. The International convention signed in Ramsar (in 1971 with the modifications of the Protocol of Paris of 1982) defines the wetlands as extensions of marshlands, swamps, peat bogs or watercovered surfaces whether they are of natural or artificial regime, temporary or permanent, stagnant or running, fresh, brackish or salty waters included on the marine water extensions whose depth in low tides shall not exceed 6 metres. The wetlands work as a water regulator and they also fulfil

signed and it means, in a word, the commitment of the states who ratified it to preserve the wetland that existed between them. France ratified this convention in 1986 and Argentina in 1991 through law 23919.[190]

298. At the same time, the fact that a site is *Ramsar* has numerous consequences pertaining to the legal and environmental field. In other words, the fact that a habitat is included before the enforcement authority of this convention – which is the International Union for Conservation of the Nature and Natural Resources – in the Wetland List of International Importance brings about the following consequences: it does not affect the sovereignty over it, the states should create natural reserves, draft and apply the planning to conserve the wetland included in the List and to their rational use. Besides, the state should inform about the modifications in the ecological conditions and their potential contamination, foster research, data exchange and publications about them.

299. The convention considered that for various urgent motives of national interest, a state can withdraw wetlands from the List, but such a behaviour must be environmentally compensated and, within their possibilities, it must create new natural reserves for those aquatic birds and for the protection of an adequate portion of their original habitat, trying to do it in the same region or in any other place.

---

biological functions positively influencing on the environment. There exist more than 1400 wetlands worldwide. In order to have access to details about Ramsar Sites in France see the work titled: *Wetlands of International Importance in France*, by Nelly Olin, former Minister of Ecology and Sustainable Development of said country.

190. This law was published in the Official Bulletin of 24 Apr. 1991. The convention defines *'aquatic birds'* as those birds that ecologically depend upon wetlands. In our country, until December 2009, there existed fourteen Ramsar sites that are: Pozuelos Lagoon (Jujuy), Río Pilcomayo National Park (Formosa), White Lagoon (Neuquén), Atlantic Coast Reserve (Tierra del Fuego), Lagoon of Yancanelo Provincial Reserve (Mendoza), Samborombón Bay (Buenos Aires), Lagoons of Guanacache (Mendoza y San Juan), Vilama Lagoon (Jujuy), Jaaukanigás Wetland (Santa Fe), The Estuaries and Lagoons of Iberá (Corrientes), Mar Chiquita Lagoon and Río Dulce wetlands (Córdoba), Laguna Brava Provincial Reserve (La Rioja), Chaco Wetlands (Chaco) and Costanera Sur Reserve (City of Buenos Aires).

Chapter 4. Agricultural Resources

§1. General Remarks

300. More than a decade ago, Argentina passed special rules on agrochemicals packaging. Resolution 350 of 1999 issued by SENASA as supplemented by Resolution 230 of 2000 of that same authority approves the manual on procedures, criteria and scopes to register phytosanitary products in Argentina. With all those Resolutions and regulations, the system tries to reach a balance between public interest and the powers to monitor the quality of the food industry and health services at phytosanitary product manufacturing facilities and private interests, and the facility owners' rights. These resolutions also refer to the research work that has to be carried out for the approval of chemicals, the suggested dosage according to crops, waiting days and toxicology.

301. As regards horticulture-related provisions, Resolution 71 of 1999 issued by the Secretary of Agriculture, Livestock, Fisheries and Foodstuff approves the hygiene and farming's good practices guideline for fresh vegetables primary production (crops), packaging, storage and transportation. This Guideline also includes suggestions on good practices as well as training, documentation and staff registration aspects and the tracing and clearing of goods from the market, in the event that hazards to human health are detected.

302. The comparison between said resolution and the comments and records made during the visits to orchards enabled the confirmation of a series of specific suggestions that are not considered in practice.

303. Currently, the SENASA- National Service on Food Safety and Quality, which depends on the Secretary of Agriculture, Fisheries and Foodstuff is the board in charge of regulating the use of fertilizers. Within this framework, the Agrochemical, Pharmaceutical and Veterinary Products Board is in charge of monitoring that the rules in force on fertilizers manufacture, trading and use, their packaging and legal labelling are accordingly complied with.

304. Being Argentina a country with similar characteristics than Australia, we believe that the conclusions reached by Byrne and Stone in their study published by Elsevier are applicable to our country. They sustain that [Australia]:

> along with other countries, is well positioned to grow and develop bio-based products from agriculture with opportunities for plant-derived bio-based products from a diversity of crops. In the mid to low rainfall regions of southern Australia such diversification of farming systems and products, driven by environmental challenges such as salinity and altered hydrological balances, has led to the development of new farming systems based around perennial species. These species and systems may be further developed to form a basis for production systems feeding the emerging bio-energy and bio-fuels markets.

Native woody species and grasses are also being investigated as sources of new bio-based products such as bio-fuels and bio-energy.[191]

305. Argentina's farming products are economically and socially paramount not only due to enormous extension of arable land in the country but also due to the existence of a rich biodiversity in its territory.

306. Due to this reason Onestini, following scientific criterion, highlights that the ecological biodiversity of the Argentine biophysical environment[192] is subject to be classified under many different categories, to wit, 'life zone' criterion, 'ecoregion' classification and 'agro productive regionalization' division. Said author stresses that 'those classification under "life zone" also include ten diverse areas; at the same time, these are divided according to some elements group such as precipitation and potential evaporation'.[193] The 'ecoregion' criterion is used by some national entities such as the SAyDS.[194] Vis-à-vis 'productive regionalization', she points out that:

> this division adds relevant composition and status for the agro production since the following are considered: geographic variables (vast geographic and ecological units, agro-productive variables (such as minor livestock, grains, subtropical farming, etc) and jurisdictional conditions of census origin.[195]

307. In the last decade, the agricultural development increased exponentially but without environmental sustainability, which produced the water cycles alterations,

---

191. Margaret Byrne & Lynley Stone, The Need for 'Duty of Care' When Introducing New Crops for Sustainable Agriculture. (*Current Opinion in Environmental Sustainability*. Issues 1–2, March Elsevier 2011), 3:50–54. Among other conclusions, the authors state that ... 'This is an important time in international agriculture, and new challenges provide an opportunity to develop innovative systems that are profitable and provide environmental benefits whilst minimizing impacts on biodiversity. Implementation of risk management policies in agricultural systems does not dictate business operating in a no-risk environment.'
192. María Onestini, *Recursos Naturales, Desarrollo Sustentable y Agricultura en Argentina*. Centro de Estudios Ambientales (CEDEA) Publishing *sine data* 2. The author highlights that 'Despite that the different environmental diagnosis do not correspond to the different biophysical classifications in Argentina, all of them admit that there is a huge ecological diversity in the territory.' On internet: www.rimisp.org/FCKeditor/UserFiles/File/documentos/docs/pdf/recursos_y_ambiente_2.pdf (accessed 31 Oct. 2011).
193. *Ibid.*, 2 quotation 1. 'The life zone classification also varies according to different authors who investigate this line of work. However, in general it is understood that in the subtropical region, the four life zones are the Misiones rainforest, Tucuman – Orense rainforest, Subtropical forest and Plateau. In the temperate warm region, the Pampas, the Mountain grazing land, the Mountain, while in the cold temperate region there are the Austral Forest, the Patagonia and the High Andean zone.'
194. According to the ecoregion criterion, the country is divided into 18 areas: The High Andes; The Plateau; Hills; Yungas Rainforests; Dry Chaco; Humid Chaco; Paranaense Rainforest; Iberá's Stuary; Fields and Weeds; Delta and Isles; The Espina, the Pampas; Hills of Plains; Patagonia Stuary; Patagonia Woods; Atlantic and Argentine Sea islands and the Antarctic.
195. Onestini highlights that according to the faming zones classification, it is divided into Plateau, North-east Valleys, irrigation areas in Santiago del Estero; Northeast subtropical agriculture; Dry Chaco, Arid Mountain; Humid Chaco, Mesopotamia; Lanar Patagonia; Cuyo and Pampas Oasis, Patagonia Valleys and Patagonia Andean Agriculture.

negative impact on health and soil erosion, among other environmentally negative consequences.[196] Onestini points out:

> the transition towards the direct sowing and the massive production of modified farming products have been one of many dynamics that have generated different agricultural processes and systems usage from the traditional ones. These tendencies, jointly with economic and trading currents, have yielded bigger pressures over some natural resources, especially since the productive changes were brought about without adequate environmental control systems.[197]

308. Since 1999, the ecological, biological and organic production relies on a specific legal regime in Argentina: law 25127 ruled by Decree 97 of 2001. This regime is completed by two other initiatives: the National Programme of Organic Production created by Decree 206 of 2001 and the National Programme of Added Value destined to Agro-industry by Decree 132 of 2009. The enforcing authority for Law 25127 is the SENASA who shall make and keep a List of Elements updated for ecologic production and is entitled to supervise the facilities, means of transport, storage and documentation.

309. This normative act provides the organic, ecological and biological classification to those systems of farming or agro-industry production including as well the collection, catching and hunting systems in time. And this system through rational handling of natural resources and avoiding the chemical synthesis products and other with real toxicity for human life must provide healthy products, keep or increase soil fertility and biological diversity, keep water resources and present and intensify soil biological cycles to provide the nutrients for vegetal and animal life and also give the necessary conditions for them to express their basic innate behaviour characteristics meeting the physiological and ecological needs.[198]

310. The product's certification regarding these requirements my be done through public or private entities authorized to do so but only those products under the 'organic', 'biological' and 'ecological' denomination can be traded and which have obtained the due SENASA authorization for said denomination.

311. Regarding organic products trading we should highlight that, in accordance with the Argentine regulation in force on trademarks and commercial designations[199] Article 10 of Decree 97 of 2001 expressly prohibits that the terms 'organic' 'biological', and 'ecological' or similar in Spanish or any other foreign

196. Onestini, *supra*, 4.
197. *Ibid.*, 3.
198. Article 1 of law 25127 of 1999.
199. Argentine Law 22362 of 1981 on Trademarks and its regulatory Decree 558 of 1981 allow the registry of a trademark under forty-five different classes, according the Nice Agreement, 9th edn. The products and services that correspond to each one of these classes may be acceded through www.estudiovillano.com.

language be brands or be part of a trademark group. Products and services trademarks previously registered to the enforcing of law 25127 are excluded.

§2. Livestock Ecosystem: Index of Natural Pastures Preservation

312. The increasing advance of plantings makes the pastures areas of Río de la Plata to diminish in size (as it is known, these pastures retain carbon in their soils and roots and delay the superficial water runoffs creating impact on the underground aquifers filtering). For those reasons, representatives of the Ministry of Environment of Paraguay, Uruguay, Brazil and the Argentine provinces of Entre Ríos, Santa Fe and Formosa joined together to form a conservationist initiative called the Pastures Alliance aiming at receiving financial aid from the Inter-American Development Bank (IDB) and establishing a common policy for natural pastures in those areas. Among its measures, we can find one aiming at studying the implementation of an Index of Natural Pastures Preservation (ICPN in Spanish) which would allow to say with absolute certainty to what extent each rural institutions contributes to the preservation of natural pastures and their ecosystem services.

§3. Rural Lands

313. On 27 December 2011 the National Law on Rural Lands No. 26737 was passed. It created the National Office of Rural Lands (where data on rural lands from foreigners is registered) and established the requirements so that foreigners (it could be legal entities or individuals whose 51% capital stock belongs to foreigners or rather is controlled by any form of social or cooperative partnership in more than 25%) become territory or rural lands owners anywhere in the country. Foreign legal entities mentioned in Article 4 of this Law shall be exempted.

The National Secretariat of Agriculture, Livestock and Fishery is the enforcement authority of said Law.

At the same time, rural lands of the same foreign owner will not be able to exceed one thousand hectares in the central zone or equivalent surface according to its geographic location.

Chapter 5. Forests

§1. General Principles

314. The general morphologic characteristics of native forests in Argentina are described by Burkart like this:

> from the six main Argentine forest ecosystems, five of them are subtropical (humid, sub-humid, and dry) and one of them is temperate. Except for the Andinean-Patagonic Forests, from the Andes Australes, the native forests in Argentina are in the Neotropical Region, in the Amazonian and Chaco Domains (Cabrera, 1994). The forest surface, estimated at 106 millions of hectares in 1914, might have reduced to some 40 millions in 1990. However, there exists some doubt about the current forest surface because many estimations place it between 35 and 45 millions of hectares (Corradini et al., 1993).[200]

315. The most recent case is that of the Salta province referred to in *Salas* (see paragraph 339 of this work) in which by a Decree the governor of said province destined a provincial reserve to soya and citric growing. This case became a matter of public opinion, and it prompted an important reaction in favour of environmental preservation by most of the community in the country.

316. Since 2006, Argentina has been already immersed in a forest emergency status, and as Machaín[201] points out:

> it has been said that if the country wants to reach the 100 millions of tons of grins, it would practically have to extend itself to the faming border between 12 and 15 millions of hectares. It can be inferred then that in the years to come we would be changing the 50% of the current native forest cover.

The deforestation resulting impacts over the ecosystems and the natural resources are multiple and of huge significance, to wit: biodiversity reduction; biomass loss; increase of the greenhouse effect and global warming; water regime alteration; reduction of the retention and infiltration capacity water among other impacts on water; increase of erosion and soil sedimentation; landscape fragmentation; fauna migration which can produce the extinction of species in the case of endemic species; increase of poaching and illegal trade of wood. The fact that replacing the forest by farming is mainly due to soya growing helps worsen this matter. Moreover,

---

200. Rodolfo Burkart, Javier García Fernández & Enrique Riegelhaupt, *Estado Actual del Uso y Conservación de Bosques Nativos en Argentina*. Fundación para la Conservación de las Especies y el Medio Ambiente, FUCEMA. Sine data. On internet: www.fucema.org.ar/old/fucema/ publicaciones/ estado_bosques1.htm (accessed 2 Nov. 2011).

201. Natalia Machaín, *La Emergencia Forestal y la Competencia Federal*, in 'Ordenamiento Territorial de Bosques Nativos', Greenpeace 2006, 7. The complete work can be read on: www.green peace.org/ raw/content/argentina/bosques/ordenamiento-territorial-de-bo.pdf (accessed 31 Oct. 2011).

even when the direct sowing is very much disseminated, there still exist farming techniques that deteriorate the soil and that finally produced desertification.

317. However, precipitation in regions where the greater advance of the faming border is taking place has turned out to be a limiting factor for agriculture. All this plus the potential soil deterioration increases the uncertainty regarding profitability and sustainability of this kind of productions in the long run. Native Argentine forests are severely degraded. They need certain treatment to foster its recovery and they need to be presented as a viable alternative of soil usage for agriculture.

§2. NATIONAL LEGISLATION

318. The applicable legal regime for Argentine forest resources consists of a specific act: the forests' wealth Law 13273 of 1948 as amended by Decree 710 of 1995, whose Appendix I organized the normative regulation, regarding this matter, that was in force. Mentioned regulations have been complemented by the recent Law 26331 of 2007 on minimum standards for environmental protection of native forests. At present, there exist projects in the national Congress to introduce modifications to them.

319. In order to show this evolution, we will first refer to the regime of forests' wealth defence and then to the law on minimum environmental standards for native forests.

§3. NATIVE FORESTS IN THE PROVINCE OF CORRIENTES

320. The province of Corrientes passed Law No. 5974 of native forests in compliance with National Law No. 26331.

Recently in that province, due to the building of a reservoir in the Ayuí River – a tributary of the Uruguay River – covering eight thousand hectares, the Ayuí Grande Protective Project was launched. Its establishment and practical consequences are being closely analysed by Valls in his article called '*El Proyecto Productivo Ayuí Grande y el Estatuto del Río Uruguay de 1975. Siguen las controversias jurídicas ambientales en la Cuenca del Plata, como ocurre desde hace quinientos años (final abierto)*' [The Ayuí Grande Productive Project and the Uruguay River's Statute from 1975. Environmental legal disputes in the Del Plata Basin are still underway as it has been happening for 500 years (open end)] published at www.eldial.com on 12 November 2012.

§4. LEGAL REGIME OF FORESTS' WEALTH DEFENCE

321. As we had said earlier, it emerges from Law 13273 of 1948 which defines forests and forests' wealth declaring 'of public utility and subject to expropriation' those forests categorized as protectors and/or permanent likely to make better use of the land, whatever its location is. Within the enforcement of this law there exist tree cases, to wit: (a) forest and forest lands located in federal jurisdiction, (b) forests and forest lands of private or public property located in those provinces that comply with the law and, (c) the protecting forests and forest lands complying with some specific conditions in Article 6, located within the province territory, provided those quality effects have an impact on the interests of the federal government.[202] This regulation categorizes forests into protectors,[203] permanent, experimental, special mountains and production forests and it states that those forests being part of the private domain of the state shall be inalienable.

322. Regarding forest exploitation, 'the forest land devastation and irrational use of forest products' is prohibited.[204] It is also prohibited for owners, usufructuaries, tenants and forest holders to start their activities provided they have due authorization of their management plan. A thirty-day period is needed for the authority to accept or deny the management plan. Likewise, in order to avoid delays in the proceedings, this law states the principle regarding legal consequences of the public administrative inaction establishing that if fifteen days have passed and the second request for the plan approval has not been answered, then it shall be considered implicitly approved.

323. The exploitation of wooded areas larger than 2,500 hectares must be carried out by dealership, with a previous public tender awarding of administration or through mixed enterprises.

324. Fiscal forest exploitation is subject to the payment of a fixed, mobile or mixed tax. It will be established bearing in mind the following: (a) species, quality and final application of the products; (b) different factors determining production cost; (c) sale prices and (d) the fostering of Argentine wood industrialization.

325. On the one hand, provinces adhering to this law have a series of obligations established by Article 4 of said law.[205]

---

202. Article 2 of Law 13273 of 1995.

203. The protector and permanent forests have a special regime because according to Arts 20 and 21 of Law 13273 of 1948, the declaration of a forest as such implies a series of taxes and restrictions, to wit: (a) to give notice in case of sale or regimen change (b) keep and reforest them in the technical conditions needed, provided that the strong reforesting be fostered by exploitation or destruction attributable to the owner (c) to carry out the possible exploitation in accordance to the technical norms approved at the owner preference; (d) to obtain previous authorization for the pasturing in the forest or for any kind of work in the soil or subsoil which may affect its existence; e) allow the forestation authority to carry out forestation and deforestation activities.

204. Article 11 of Law 13273 of 1948 establishes a common forest regime for those forests ruled by this norm.

205. Said obligations belong to institutional, economic and tax reasons and they comprise: (a) the creation of provincial agency in charge of the enforcement of that present law (b) the creation of a forest provincial fund, on the basis of fruit and natural forest products taxes coming from the province's general budget; (c) to extend the federal forest regime in the provincial jurisdiction and administer its forests according to this regime (d) grant tax exemptions set forth in the Arts 40 and 41; (e) coordinate municipal and provincial agencies' functions and services in charge of forest preservation and promotion together with the federal forest authorization; (f) coordinate together

326. The norm includes a special chapter about fire prevention and a penal regime according to which the following actions are considered forests violations, to wit: (a) take or produce fire inside forests or neighbouring areas violating the respective rules; (b) to pull up, destroy or damage trees and take out sap and resin violating the respective rules; (c) destroy, remove or suppress signs or indicators, barb wires, posters or refugees placed by the forest authority; (d) any violation of the approved exploitation plan; (e) disobey orders under legal and regulatory norms; (f) to falsify reports; (g) to omit the complaint expressed in Article 34; (h) any other violation to the present law and decrees, resolutions, dispositions or instructions passed consequently; (i) and introduce livestock in violation of the forest land and forests regulations.

327. Articles 51 and 53 of said law establish procedure norms to be followed. The fines amount from ARS 20,000 to ARS 100,000 and may be imposed without detriment of civil and criminal actions that may apply.

328. In order to promote the forest activities development and woods exploitation, a law granting fiscal stability to those activities has been passed.[206] This stability lasts thirty-three years from the presentation date of the respective feasibility project. It is granted to those companies exclusively developing forest activities and in practical terms, it means that companies developing forest activities or reducing the exploitation of forests shall not have its tax burden affected with rises in tax contributions and national, provincial or municipal tax, or the creation of new ones. This is national regime and is applicable to those provinces adhering to it and it excludes the VAT, the employer's contributions and the customs taxes.

§5. Regime of Minimum Environmental Standards for Native Woods

329. This regime was passed by Law 26331 of 2007, which establishes, apart from minimum standards for environmental protection, a promotion and criteria regime for the fund's distribution for environmental services[207] that native forests provide. The Appendix in this law establishes environmental sustainability criteria for the territorial planning of native forests. The enforcing authority at a federal level is the SAyDS. It also determines the correspondent jurisdiction in the provinces and in the city of Buenos Aires. This law is ruled by Decree 91 of 2009.

---

with the federal forest authority the forestation and deforestation plans and the exploitation of fiscal, provincial or communities forests, especially when related to the specific moment to carry these activities out, total sum of inspections or exploitation rights; (g) adopt the regime on s. V of said law for the fiscal forests in its jurisdiction.

206. The norm providing fiscal stability of these activities is law 24857 of 1997.

207. Intangible and tangible benefits are environmental services generated by the native forest ecosystems needed for the harmony and survival of the natural and biological system as a whole and to enhance and assure the quality of life for the inhabitants of the Nation. Art. 5 of this law states that particularly they are: water regulation, biodiversity conservation, soil and quality of water conservation, the fixation of greenhouse gases emissions, contribution to the beauty of landscapes and the defence of the cultural identity.

330. This norm contains a number of definitions that are useful for its understanding and application. For example, it defines native forests as those:

> natural forest ecosystems predominantly made up of mature native trees species with diverse flora and fauna species, together with their surroundings – soil, subsoil, atmosphere, climate, water resources-, creating a interdependent weft with its own characteristics and multiple functions, which in its natural state provides the system with a dynamic balance condition and diverse environmental services to society and the diverse natural resources with an economic objective.

Said concept comprises forests where there man did not intervened ('primary') and those formed alter a voluntary clearing or recovery ('secondary') excluding all exploitation in surfaces minor to 10 hectares that are indigenous communities' property or small producers.

331. This law also defines the concepts of 'clearing' and 'sustainable management'. Clearing is 'any anthropogenic activity that makes the forest loses its own natural characteristics producing the conversion of its soil use to other uses: agriculture, livestock, forestation, dam constructions or urban areas developments'.[208] Sustainable management is defined as:

> the organization, administration, native forest use in such a way and intensity that may allow to maintain its biodiversity, productivity, vitality, potentiality and regeneration capacity to consider now and in the future the ecologic, economic and social relevant functions in the local and national levels without making damage to other ecosystems and keeping the Environmental Services for society.[209]

Since 2009, the SAyDS counts on an Experimental Programme on Management and Conservation of Native Forests, passed by Resolution 256 SAyDS of 2009.

332. Within the context of this law, three native forest conservation categories are established, to wit, red, yellow and green according to conservation values such as high, intermediate or low, respectively.

333. Upon this law, a National Programme for Native Forest Protection is created. It functions within the SAyDS jurisdiction and one of its functions is to apply recovery, exploitation and ordering measures.

334. The burning of the clearing and exploitation waste is strictly forbidden.[210] The category I clearing (red) and II (yellow) are also prohibited, while for category

---

208. Article 4 of Law 26331 of 2007.
209. Article 4 of Law 26331 of 2007.
210. Further regulations related to burning activities are contained in Law 26562 of 2009, as we explain in §6 of this chapter.

III (green) an Exploitation Plan of Soil use change must be presented.[211] It must consider 'the minimum conditions for sustainable production in the short, intermediate and long-term and the use of certain available technologies that allow efficient performance',[212] and also the indigenous communities' rights of that place. Said plan must be approved by the enforcing authority of the forest jurisdiction previous to the beginning of the activities.

335. The EIA, whose regime comes from Articles 22 and 25 of this law, is mandatory to the clearing while it is also mandatory for the sustainable management provided the project can bring about significant impacts. Also, those projects that have the following characteristics are considered mandatory as well, to wit: adverse significant changes on the renewable resources' quantity and quality included in the soil, water, and air; the new settlement of human communities or significant alterations in the life systems and human groups habits; near location to population, protected resources or areas likely to be affected, and the environmental value of the territory where the project is thought to be carried out; significant alterations of the landscape or tourist area in terms of its magnitude or duration and those monuments of anthropologic, archaeological, historical value and those belonging to cultural heritage. The requirements for the Environmental Impact Study are described in Article 24 of this law.

336. For clearing projects, the enforcing authority must guarantee the hearing mechanisms and public consult established in the General Law for Environment 25675 of 2002, and in the Regime for Access to the Public Environmental Information (explained in the Introduction §4. II of this work) ruled by law 25831 of 2004 when applicable.

337. This normative frame is completed with a penal regime that considers the creation of a National Registry for environmental offenders[213] under the SAyDS' jurisdiction. This registers any private or public person that was a forest or 'environmental' regime offender either national or provincial[214] provided the sanctions imposed were not enforced. Those enrolled in said Registry should not be holders of any clearing or sustainable exploitation authorization.

338. The law establishes the obligation of previous administrative summary proceedings that is carried out in the jurisdiction where the offence was caused. Sanctions regarded in this national law are disciplinary measures, a fine of 300–10,000 basic salaries of the first category of the National Public Administration and

211. The Exploitation Plan must be subscribed by an entitled professional. In the case of 'present or future environmental damage related to data falsehood or omission' of the Exploitation Plan 'those persons who subscribed the studies' are responsible jointly and severally with the holder of the authorization. (Art. 20 of Law 26331 of 2007).
212. Article 15 of Law 26331 of 2007.
213. Data and details with the information that each local jurisdiction should provide to this national registry can be found in Annex A of Resolution 514 of 2009 of SAyDS.
214. Article 27 Law 26331.

suspension of the authorization. Jurisdictions lacking a penal regime are entitled to apply this specific one.

339. As regards the national penal regime, doctrine has pointed out that if the regime is infringed and (in terms of Corrientes province in particular) there are:

> two hypothetical situations that ultimately involve the same punishment as they are not segregated: (1) Clearing of native forests after submitting, to the enforcing authority, a management plan regarding a Land Clearing Project, but without receiving authorization thereof; (2) Clearing of native forests without submitting any management plan regarding a Land Clearing Project. With these two hypothetic situations, it is shown that the Native Forest enforcing Authority is unable to enforce sanctions.[215]

340. Likewise, this regime plans the creation of a National Fund for the Native Forest Enrichment and Conservation and the resources and the guideline on administration and application upon which it will be created.[216]

§6. Promotional Investment Regime

341. National Law 25080 was enacted in 1999 and created a special investment regime for cultivated forests. This law was partially modified by law 26432 of 2008. It defines cultivated forest as those forests obtained through the sowing and planting of native wood and/or exotic species ecologically adapted to the place with mainly commercial and industrial purposes in lands where due to their natural conditions, location and aptitude are susceptible to forestation or deforestation according to what is indicated in the territorial act of native Forests adopted by the provincial law in the context of law 26331 of 2007, which sets forth the minimum environmental standards for native forests protection.

342. This law grants tax benefits among which we can mention the fiscal stability for a thirty year term that may be extended until fifty years, the returning of due amount of the Valued Added Tax (VAT) and a series of alternatives for those who recoup the income tax and 'a non-reimbursable financial support to those established forests' that the state grants through a single payment to the beneficiaries.[217]

---

215. Daniel Fernando Segovia, *Regimen sancionatorio en materia de bosques nativos de la Nación Argentina y la provincia de Corrientes*. Published at www.eldial.com.ar on 4 Oct. 2011 (accessed 18 Nov. 2011).

216. In 2010, under the auspices of the National Park Administration, Marcela Lunazzi (coordinator) & Valeria Rodríguez (coordinator) prepared the *Guidelines to Prepare Protected Areas Management Plans*. Their goal is to unify the criteria to prepare management plans. Its three chapters deal with planning, management plans and preparation criteria, as well as the management plans concepts and contents and the steps and stages to prepare and/or update management plans.

217. The economic support is granted on the basis of the following scale: (a) From 1 to 300 hectares up to 80% of establishment expenses; (b) From 301 to 500 hectares up to (20%) of the establishment

The enforcing authority is the Secretariat of Agriculture, Livestock, Fishery and Foodstuff. There existed a Follow-up Commission of said law in the national Congress of the country.

§7. Control of Burning Activities

343. The minimum environmental protection standards for burning activities in the whole country are specifically regulated by Law 26562 of 2009. Although this norm has not been reglamented yet, it is in force. It was enacted to prevent fire, environmental damage, health and public security risks.

344. The norm defines 'burning' as every 'vegetation or vegetation waste elimination through the use of fire, with the aim of obtaining a permit for a productive exploitation of a land.'[218] As we can see, it is a reprehensible definition, since it requires a two-fold intentional element – the aim of 'commissioning land' and that it should be done so for 'its productive exploitation'- which will very probably restrict, practically speaking, its application possibilities due to the lack of accreditation of *both* intentional elements. From both requirements, we consider that 'productive exploitation' will bring about significant difficulties of effective control, since the declaration about having carried out certain activities to make use, for example, of a building as a temporary warehouse for working elements of their own, will hamper the restrictions enforcement considered by this regime.

345. This is so without considering that this law states that local enforcing authorities 'should set up conditions and requirements to authorize the burning' which should contemplate 'at least, climatic, seasonal, regional, soil, flora and fauna preservation parameters, as well as technical requirements so as to prevent the risk of spread of fire and safeguard health and public security'.[219]

346. This law bans the non-specific authorization burning and empowers the local authorities to establish banned burning zones and stop the authorized burnings when the meteorological conditions 'or of any other kind of conditions' may imply 'serious' or 'fire danger' risks.[220] If the burning is authorized in a land adjoining two jurisdictions, the authority that had granted the burning permit must notify the other competent authority of said adjoining jurisdiction about the tasks that will be carried out.

347. The burning permit request must contain the following requirements: data of the person in charge of the land exploitation, data of the holder of the property,

---

expenses. In the Patagonian Region the subsidy set forth regimen will be extended; (c) To 500 hectares up to (80%) of the establishment expenses; (d) To 700 hectares up to (20%) of the establishment expenses.

218. Article 2 of Law 26562 of 2009.
219. Article 4, Law 26562 of 2009.
220. Articles 4–5, Law 26562 of 2009.

consent of the holder, identification of the land where the burning will take place, aim of the burning and description of the vegetation and/or vegetation waste that wants to be disposed of, the techniques that will be adopted for the burning, control and fire extinction, prevention measures and the security that will be implemented in order to prevent the spread of fire and safeguard health and public security, date and hour set for the beginning and end of the burning as exact as possible.[221]

348. This law, faithful to its minimum standards' regime nature, disregards the sanctions for those cases that failed to comply empowering local authorities to set and apply them. However, and until it happens to be, it establishes the following penalties: a fine of about ARS 50 – ARS 10,000 similar to the basic salaries of the national public service and banning for the offender to carry out future burnings. Said sanctions will be imposed without the detriment of the corresponding ones in case of having to impose those special norms regarding forests, that is, the defence of forests' wealth defence Law 13273 of 1948 as amended by Decree 710 of 1995, and Law 26331 of 2007 on minimum standards for environmental protection of native forests.

§8. Recent Relevant Cases: Native Forests in Salta Province

349. The Argentine Supreme Court of Justice sentenced a case in November 2010 where the national University of Salta promoted a declarative action of certainty arguing that absolute and insane nullity was in the Salta's provincial Law 7543 because it allegedly damaged the constitutional rights and guarantees of indigenous and rural communities inhabiting that particular area. The national Supreme Court disagreed on the plaintiff's arguments and declared its jurisdiction to the initiated action.[222]

350. In re *Salas,* there was a discussion over clearing in forbidden areas of the province of Salta. The CSJN had adopted a provisional measure that included the clearing suspension in the province of Salta, focusing on the precautionary principle established by national Law 25675 of 2002, the so-called General Law on the Environment. In addition, the High Court dictated the refusal of the possibility of any independent agency of dimensioning the damage caused by the illegal clearings during the validity of the measure since the magnitude of said activity could only eventually bring about claims related to damaging consequences of said activity. This would exceed the context of this process and would be alien to mentioned Court's jurisdiction, established by Article 117 of the national Constitution.[223]

221. Article 6 of Law 26562 of 2009.
222. Sentence published by Doctrina Judicial La Ley, año 26, nº 7, 17 Feb., 2011 353.
223. See *Salas, Dino y otros v. Salta y Estado Nacional sobre Amparo* decided by the Supreme Court of Justice on 14 Sep. 2010. www.eldial.com/bases/sql/ver_rl_tttNP.asp?base=14&id=26367 (accessed 4 Oct. 2010.

Chapter 6. Subsoil and Minerals

§1. Introduction

351. A total of nineteen sedimentary basins with a total surface of nearly 1,750,000 km^2 have been identified in Argentina, out of which, five continue on the continental shelf, while three extend below sea level. The onshore basins surface is of 1,350,000 km^2, while the ocean basins' surface, considering the iso-line of 200 metres as a limit, is of 400,000 km^2. This latter figure may be doubled if the surface is calculated up to the slope's bottom. There are currently five basins that produce hydrocarbons, to wit: the Northeast, Cuyana, Neuquén, San Jorge Gulf and Austral or Magallanes basins. If the portion above sea level is the only one considered, its surface represents 40% of what is currently known as oil basins. From 1907 through 1985, 24400 wells have been concluded in the country; 22.5% thereof are barren wells, while the remaining ones are productive: there are 17466 oil wells and 1457 natural gas wells that amount to 18,923 wells or 77.5% thus showing a high efficiency level.[224,225]

352. At sea, the oil activities are mainly carried out in sedimentary basins, subsoil areas with thick layers of sediment that can produce and store hydrocarbons. The argentine continental margin includes ten sedimentary basins of different lengths.

One of them, the Austral Basin, includes the only productive oilfields. This *offshore* prospecting is located in front of the north coast of Tierra del Fuego province.[226]

§2. Hydrocarbon Exploration, Prospecting and Production

353. In the 1970s, it was considered that the Río de la Plata subsoil could have hydrocarbon reservoirs. This idea triggered the 1973 agreement between Argentina and Uruguay: the Treaty on Río de la Plata and its Maritime Front, still in force. Argentina adopted said treaty through Law 20645 of 1973. It sets forth the limits as

224. Information as officially provided by the Secretary of Energy. Official web site: http://energia3.mecon.gov.ar/contenidos/verpagina.php?idpagina=815 (accessed 7 Nov. 2011.
225. In November 2011 the oil company YPF, the biggest corporation in Argentina, announced an important hydrocarbon discovery. 'The exploration results of the first area, comprising 428 km2 in La Lata, show recoverable resources of 927 million in oil barrels, 741 million of which pertain to oil barrels and the remaining amount to gas barrels. The Spanish-argentine giant, ensuring that it is "the largest oil discovery in history" stated that this first discovery is "similar to YPF current proved reserves" and that they can significantly increase'. This is an article published by Clarín, which is available at www.ieco.clarin.com/empresas/YPF-anuncio-importante-descubrimiento-petrolero_0_586741545.html (accessed 7 Nov. 2011.
226. Source *Manual de Intereses Marítimos Argentinos*, published by the Navy's Secretary of Marine Interests. Internet web site: www.ara.mil.ar/archivos/Docs/IIMM-02-Capitulo%202.pdf (accessed 7 Nov. 2011.

well as the provisions on the river's administration, and environmental,[227] navigation, work activities and fishing-related issues. The treaty is applicable to two geographically different areas: the 'Río de la Plata' and its 'Maritime Front'.

354. Both the Argentine Mining Code (in Article 7)[228] and the Civil Code (in Article 2342, subsection 2)[229] set forth the same governing principle: mines are private goods belonging to the national government or the provinces, depending on their location. Said principle was firmly maintained until the 1949 amendment to the NC, whereby provinces transferred ownership to the national government and it was then considered that the national government held an inalienable and imprescriptible right to minerals, waterfalls, oilfields and natural gas deposits and other energy sources with the pertinent profit-sharing as agreed upon with the provinces. This amendment was then rendered ineffective.

355. Today, and as it was already explained in this work, Article 124 of the NC – as amended in 1994 – states that provinces have the ownership of the natural resources within their territory.[230]

356. But in Argentina, the ownership of natural resources does not essentially mean jurisdiction over them. The CSJN has stated that 'the terms ownership and jurisdiction are neither equivalent nor correlative terms because they are independent'.[231]

357. Therefore, the current legal situation regarding hydrocarbons is the following: their ownership rests in the provinces but it is the national Congress that has the exclusive power to enact substantive laws thereon (Mining Code) and regulate the legal relationships arising from their use. This split has been severely criticized by legal doctrine experts[232] although it was ratified by several CSJN rulings.[233]

---

227. See Freplata's excellent study *Programa de Acción Ambiental Estratégica para la Protección Ambiental del Río de la Plata y su Frente Marítimo. Revisión de Legislación y Propuestas para Armonización* on environmental regulations, in which the distinguished Argentine Professor María Cristina Zeballos de Sisto participated as consultant. The complete text of this study is available on Internet at the following web site: www.freplata.org/documentos/archivos/Documentos_Freplata/Legislacion.pdf (accessed 5 Nov. 2011).
228. This Article sets forth that 'The mines are private goods of the nation or the provinces depending on where they are located.'
229. According to this subsection, the national governments' and provinces' private goods include 'gold, silver, copper, precious stones and fossil substances. This is determined regardless of the individuals and companies ownership of land'.
230. During the discussions at the Constitutional Convention, the possible transfer of the jurisdiction to provinces was considered but the decision died therein. See the Constitutional Convention's Journal, Meeting 28, 3° Ordinary Session, 10 and 11 Aug. 1994, 3871. Quoted by Cassagne, among others, in his study *La Propiedad de los Yacimientos de Hidrocarburos. Su Relación con las Potestades Nacionales y Provinciales*. La Ley 2007, C, 1243.
231. National Supreme Court of Justice, CSJN Fallos 154:312.
232. Said inconsistency was highlighted by specialized experts in mining law doctrine. They stated that 'there are no records on provincial goods, whose final destiny is limited to any restriction whatsoever'. See Edmundo F. Catalano, *Código de Minería Comentado* (Buenos Aires: Zavalía, 1999), 76.
233. CSJN Fallos 301:341.

358. In line with the current Article 124 of the NC the National Executive Power has issued Decree 546 of 2003 by means of which it granted three essential powers to the provinces: the power to prepare bid conditions, the power to act as an enforcing authority of the Hydrocarbons Law in terms of the hydrocarbon permits and concessions granted by each of them and the power to solve disputes arising from said concessions within the framework of the guidelines set forth under said decree. However, that same decree states that the national government has the exclusive right to determine the national policy regarding hydrocarbons and to regulate the hydrocarbon prospecting, exploration and transportation activities.[234]

359. In 2006 Law 26197 was passed. Its enforcing authority is the Secretary of Energy and the law reaffirms the criterion set forth under Article 124 of the NC as it expressly determines that 'all the hydrocarbon exploration permits and prospecting concessions are fully transferred together with any hydrocarbon exploration and/or prospecting agreement either subscribed or approved by the National Government in exercise of its powers, without affecting the permit and concession holders rights and duties'. The royalties shall be determined according to the legislation in force and shall be granted to the jurisdictions where the oilfields and deposits are located.[235]

360. This law also includes the hydrocarbons located in the argentine continental shelf. Indeed, the law sets forth that the hydrocarbon wells located 12 miles as from the baselines set forth under Law 23968 of 1991, to the continental shelf edge, belong to the national government, while those located in the provinces and the adjacent waters to 12 nautical miles belong to the latter. Following the governing criterion, and despite no practical application thereof, the law establishes that the wells located in the city of Buenos Aires belong to it.

361. Later on and given the probable existence of hydrocarbon wells in the Buenos Aires province adjacent waters, Law 26197 of 2007 was passed. It accordingly determines that the wells located in the Río de la Plata bed and subsoil, up to 12 nautical miles, belong to the Buenos Aires province or the city of Buenos Aires. As regards the country's southern area, this law also determines that the hydrocarbon wells located in Tierra del Fuego province to 12 nautical miles belong to it.

362. In sum, and as Professor Gelli explains:

> Law 26197 on the provinces administration of the hydrocarbons wells starts ruling that these solid or liquid wells inalienably and imprescriptibly belong to the national jurisdiction or the provinces according to where they are located . The law also determined, since its enactment, that the provinces have full ownership of said resource as well as the administration of the wells. It also stated

234. The distribution and transportation of natural gas is governed by Law 24076 of 1992.
235. Article 2 of Law 26197 of 2007.

that said situation will not affect the exploration permit and prospection concession holders' rights and duties.[236]

363. The exploration permits and prospecting concessions are granted by bids, and any person who meets the requirements set forth under Article 5 of Law 26197 of 2007 and the selection procedure under Article 5 of said law (Articles 45–55) may participate. Those permits and concessions may be assigned to the successful bidders with the Executive Power's prior authorization. Law 26197 of 2007 also determines the applicable punishments and the administrative review remedy in case of default and includes a Single Appendix detailing the areas initially reserved for exploration and prospecting by state-owned companies.

364. In a nutshell, it may be said that the exploration permits are granted on a case-by-case basis for four years[237], and give their holders the exclusive right to carry out geological and geophysical studies as well as the right to use 'other methods' for oil exploration. The activities include preparing blueprints, carrying out studies and land and geodetic surveys and any and all other tasks or works authorized by law. The exploration permits are only applicable 'in viable areas'. As regards the dimensions, the law determines that the exploration unit comprises 100 km^2 and up to 100 exploration unit permits can be granted.[238] No person can be a direct or indirect holder of more than five exploration permits.

365. Upon expiration of the term, the essential data gathered during the surface recognition must be delivered to the enforcing authority, which can prepare them per se or through third-parties and use them as it deems convenient. Nevertheless, during the two following years, it shall not be entitled to disclose them, unless the interested party expressly authorizes said disclosure or permits or concessions in the area are granted. The permits give rise to several duties such as the duty to define the area, to carry out the necessary activities to locate hydrocarbons with 'due diligence and according to the most efficient techniques' and make the minimum investments agreed in the application.[239]

366. The prospecting concessions grant the exclusive right of prospecting wells for twenty-five years 'as from the date of the resolution granting said right' together with any additional concession that may apply, according to Article 23 of Law 26197 of 2007. These concessions may be extended for up to ten years.

367. Furthermore, and as Corró explains particularly regarding the oil activities developed in the continent during prospecting, gravimetry, satellite studies,

236. María Angélica Gelli, *supra*, v. 1, 615.
237. The different maximum period by which prospection permits and eventual extensions can be granted are established by Art. 23 of Law 26197 of 2007. The period for the permits may be expanded for one year when the activities are carried out in the Argentine continental shelf.
238. Exploration permits on up to 150 units may be granted regarding the continental shelf.
239. Article 20, Law 26197 of 2007.

magnetometry and seismic activity, are not significant from the negative environmental impact standpoint when they are used as tools to analyse or study the surface.[240]

368. Conversely, oil prospecting causes a problem 'with two significant aspects. On the one hand, the spread in the land, which may increase the oil spill risk and on the other hand, the saltpetre that is highly pollutant and thus must be carefully managed, especially if it is created in large amounts'. The author mentions other factors with less environmental impact: venting of gas and waste appearing at the bottom of the storage tanks 'as a result of the decantation of solid particles that accumulate in the oil containers floors'.[241] Corró's clarifying work details the different impacts of the offshore hydrocarbon exploration and prospecting activities on the marine environment.[242]

369. In the refineries where the crude oil is separated from the different by-products for trading purposes, Corró finds another specific environmental problem: 'the large amount of waste that is generated due to gas, liquid effluent and solid waste emissions apart from their noises, smells and other aesthetic impact' and she adds 'that gas emissions may have local, regional (acid rain) and global (green house effect) effects.'[243]

370. In terms of legislation, in 1995 the national Congress enacted Law 24585 that includes supplementary provisions in the Mining Code under the title 'Environmental Protection for the Mining activity'. It regulates the protection of the environment, and the natural and cultural heritage that may be affected by mining activities. This law applies to individuals, public and private companies and decentralized agencies that carry out mineral prospecting, exploration, exploitation, development, preparation, and drilling and storage activities. The closing of the mine and triturating, melting and polishing activities and others that may result from new technologies, including waste disposal, are expressly included therein. The law determines that the mining right holder and the person authorized by him to exercise such right shall be jointly liable. It is mandatory to submit an Environmental Impact Report to receive a DEI that shall be updated every two years at most. For the exploration stage, the Report shall include a description of the methods to be used and the environmental protection measures that are deemed necessary. No activity can be started without the prior approval of the Report.

371. Articles 19–21 determine that the administrative summary proceedings are mandatory before any punishment is applied. These punishments may include warnings, fines, suspension of the Certificate of Environmental Quality, repair of

---

240. Lucrecia Corró *Environmental Impact*. S/L S/D. See this excellent study, particularly regarding title 3.1 *Problemática ambiental asociada a la exploración petrolera*, 230 et seq. Available on Internet www.ingenieroambiental.com/3020/reparacionambiental.pdf (accessed 7 Nov. 2011).
241. *Problemática ambiental asociada a la exploración petrolera*, 253 et seq.
242. *Ibid.*, 236 et seq.
243. *Ibid.*, 240 et seq.

environmental damages, the temporary closure and disqualification, depending on the offence and the damage caused.

372. It must be pointed out that the mitigation and prevention of environmental impacts resulting from hydrocarbon exploration and prospecting are particularly governed by the 'Rules and Procedures' on environmental protection as approved by Appendix I of Resolution 195 of 1992 issued by the Secretary of Energy.

373. This Resolution follows the guidelines set forth by the *Instituto Argentino de Petróleo* and its application is mandatory for the company performing said activities in the national jurisdiction. This Resolution determines that, during the exploration stage and before the first well is drilled, it is mandatory to submit an 'Environmental Study of Advance' to determine the suggestions to prevent and reduce the environmental impact that the drilling may cause. Mentioned 'Study' is paramount to enable the governing authority to carry out the environmental monitoring tasks together with provincial authorities.

374. If the well is under a prospecting stage, the annual monitoring of every work and tasks shall be performed to protect the environment, the resources of the area and the area of influence where said activities are carried out.

375. According to this regulation, the 'Environmental Study of Advance' must include the environmental impacts caused by camps, roads and paths, the prevention measures related to the use of explosives and seismic wells, the environmental studies for the drilling and exploration stages, the actions to be taken upon the abandonment of the affected land once the exploration activities have been concluded, the storage of fuel, batteries and waste of environmental management, the rules on water collection and the environmental laws to comply during the following stage, that is to say, during the development or production stages.

376. After Resolution 195 of 1992 was passed by the Secretary of Energy, several environmental provisions related to the hydrocarbon exploration, prospecting and production activities were adopted. The most relevant provisions include the Rules to Submit Environmental Studies related to the Hydrocarbon Exploration Permits and Prospecting Concessions,[244] the Rules on Reconditioning Pools and Restoring Soil,[245] the Rule governing Contingency Plans and the Duty to Report Incidents that may affect Natural and/or the Socio-Economic Value Resources,[246] the Annual Working Plan for New Pipelines, Gas Pipelines, Multi Purpose Pipelines and Supplementary Facilities[247] and the Rules on Reporting Important Environmental Incidents Affecting Human, Socio-Economic and Natural Resources.[248]

244. Approved by Resolution 25 of 2004 issued by the Secretariat of Energy. This Resolution replaces Resolution 252 of 1993 of the Secretariat of Energy, which adopted the Guidelines and Recommendations to Develop the Environmental Studies set forth under Resolution 195 of 1992.
245. Approved by Resolution 341 of 1993 of the Secretariat of Energy.
246. Approved by Resolution 5 of 1996 of SETyC.
247. Approved by Provision 19 of 2004 of SSC.
248. Approved by Resolution 24 of 2004 of the Secretariat of Energy.

Part III. Zoning and Land-Use Planning

§1. Introduction

377. Argentine land-use planning has a very poor practical relation with environmental policies. This is so, even though national legislation obliges the environmental rules be generated through inter-jurisdictional coordination[249] between agreed rules among local counties and provinces, and between the latter and the city of Buenos Aires through the COFEMA. In the very heart of this Board, the harmonizing of the different social sectors' interests among them is considered as well as the latter with the public service. The territorial codes processes must guarantee the properly environmental use of the natural resources, the highest production and usage of the different ecosystems, the minimum degradation and 'the social participation in instrumental decisions on sustainable development'.[250]

378. Especially, from the housing point of view, the country has a very big deficit which, in the last decades, has generated an exponential growth of new poor urban settlements in big cities' surrounding zones, and especially in the Metropolitan Area of Great Buenos Aires (AMBA as per its acronym in Spanish).[251]

Regarding that problem, Law 25675 of 2002 with its teaching nature states that in the location of urban settlements the:

> following must be primarily taken into account: (a) every region or area tendency in terms of its environmental resources and its social, economic and ecologic sustainability; (b) population distribution and its particular features; (c) nature and the particular features of the different biomass; (d) the existing biomass alterations emerging from urban settlements, economic activities or any other human activity or natural phenomena and, (e) the protection and preservation of those significant ecosystems.[252]

---

249. Said actions are set by Art. 9 of Law 25675 of 2002.
250. These are the principles set by Art. 10 of law 25675 of 2002.
251. The Board of Control of the Management of National Fund for Housing (FONAVI) drafted a report titled *FONAVI: Viviendas y Soluciones Habitacionales Terminadas – Período 1976/2009* with details, province by province, in that period. On internet: www.vivienda.gov.ar/docestadisticas.php (accessed 13 Nov. 2011).
252. Article 10 of Law 25675 of 2002.

§2. JURISDICTION AND APPLICABLE LEGISLATION

379. Being Argentina a federal state, the urban planning at a national level is virtually non-existent since it is developed in an agreed-by-consensus way in the COFEMA. In certain cases, the municipalities have to pass regulations on the urban soil usage, as we saw in paragraph 367 of this work. From a regulatory point of view, Article 8 Law 25675 of the National Environmental Policy states that the environmental regulation of the territory is one the six instruments of the environmental policy and management.[253] Currently, there are various social programmes funded by the national state among which The Federal Programme of Housing Emergency can be found. This programme attempts at dealing with the housing and working problem thus organizing those unemployed allowance beneficiaries into working cooperatives for the construction of houses.

380. In the city of Buenos Aires, up to 1997, there was no Planning Code, which was then adopted in the said year. The city only had a Building Code dated as of 1944 – which had numerous modifications- in which there were restrictions to have multi-storey buildings. It was then in 2009 when the Legislative body of the city of Buenos Aires passed the Environmental Urban Plan through the enforcement of Law 2930. In Appendix I of said law, a working document titled 'Diagnosis of the city' was adopted thus giving birth to the Environmental Urban Plan.[254]

381. At present, the city of Buenos Aires has a series of Codes that govern the environmental aspects in a scattered way. Such normative elements are The Urban Planning Code, the Contamination Prevention Code, the Building Code[255] and the Authorization and Verification Code, apart from a series of environmental laws for specific purposes. According to the Environmental Urban Plan (adopted in 2009 by Law 2930), all those norms must be drawn up again in four normative acts: An Urban Code, An Environmental Code, a Building Code and an Authorization and Verification Code.[256] The Environmental Urban Plan implementation is carried out by the Board of the Environmental Urban Plan. Said agency should also deal with environmental and territorial and management priorities.[257] The administration of

253. The remaining five instruments that Art. 8 mentions are: environmental impact assessment, the system for the control of the anthropogenic activities development, the environmental education, the diagnosis and environmental information system and the economic regime of sustainable development promotion.
254. The documents, as well as the Final Text, Antecedents, Report and Participative Document of said Environmental Urban Plan can be read on internet in the official web site of the Commission for Environmental Urban plan (CoPUA) under the authority of the government of the city of Buenos Aires. See www.buenosaires.gov.ar/areas/planeamiento_obras/copua/plan_urbano_ ambiental.php (accessed 15 Nov. 2011).
255. Building Code for the City of Buenos Aires, available on the following official web site: http://estatico.buenosaires.gov.ar/areas/jef_gabinete/comision_decreto_1332/cuerpo_codigo_edificacion.pdf (accessed 13 Nov. 2011).
256. Article 24 of Law 2930 of 2009 establishes the normative criteria that new aforementioned Codes must comply with and which regulate building and the form of use of the city of Buenos Aires.
257. Article 29 of Law 2930 of 2009 sets out mentioned priorities.

the Board of the Environmental Urban Plan is controlled by the General Audit of the city of Buenos Aires.

382. In the province of Buenos Aires' jurisdiction, the constitution was amended in 1994 but said amendment did not grant town councils independence regarding the soil usage. In said province, there coexist twenty-four town councils and the city of Buenos Aires, which, at the same time, is the federal capital city of the country.

383. Due to its location in the undulating Pampas in the province of Buenos Aires, it does not present those serious problems as other Latin American cities have, where some mountain slides exist (such as Quito and Caracas), but it there exist some controversies vis-à-vis population, productive activities and the natural environment.

In this province, many agencies are devoted to urban and environmental aspects since many decades.[258]

§3. Links between Land-Use and Zoning Law and Environmental Law

384. As a backbone document on this subject matter, we can refer to the Methodology Guide for Urban Planning Surveys drafted in February 2000 by the Undersecretary's office of Urban Development and Housing, under the authority of the Secretary Office of Public Works of the current Department for Federal Planning, Public Investments and Services of the Nation.[259] It is a document regarding the classifications of basic concepts vis-à-vis urban problems and the methodology framework definition for the orientation of the urban development process.

385. This document is divided into chapters. The first one introduces clarifying definitions, technical terms, a description of the planning levels and their relationship with the surveys' application and a technical/administrative organization scheme for the urban plans implementations. The second chapter refers to the urban planning process and has a detailed description of each and every step within a global scheme that allows the feedback of said process. The third chapter aims at achieving the most possible unification in the graphical documentations, the correct nomenclature and the format for the surveys presentation in whole. Besides, a chapter with a practical example was included, through a theoretical model explained systematically. The graphic elements expressing each one of the planning process stages can also be seen.

386. There was the intention of completing the document by adding appendixes with concrete examples of plans in the country but it has not been done so, yet.

258. Nora Clichevsky. *Pobreza y Políticas Urbano-Ambientales en Argentina*. Comisión Económica para América Latina (CEPAL – ECLAC), 14. Santiago de Chile. 2002. This document can be read on Internet on: www.eclac.org/publicaciones/xml/0/10560/lcl1720_1.pdf (accessed 13 Nov. 2011).
259. Available online: www.herrera.unt.edu.ar/urbanismo2/u2/guiaplaneamientourbano.pdf (accessed 13 Nov. 2011).

Part IV. Liability Questions

Chapter 1. Introduction

387. As Laura van der Meer[260] explains when she compares the environmental liability regimes in Canada, Nepal, the Philippines, Poland and Argentina analysing the differences between sector-specific environmental liability regimes and 'general systems, which provide for liability and redress for damages to biodiversity of the environment, regardless of the source of harm', even though national liability regimes differ one from each other, it is clear that 'some provisions are standard in almost all existing liability legislation'. Indeed, and after having reviewed nineteen different regimes mentioned author finds out that the common features include: the definition of damage, provisions of threshold for triggering the application of liability rules, that liability is channelled to the 'owner' of the 'operator', and different types of liabilities, among other features.

388. Also at the international level, Gunningham highlighted, after having examined the evolution of environmental law, regulation and governance over almost four decades, that 'environmental law and policy has come a long way since the birth of the US Environmental Protection Agency in 1970 and the launch of the first European environmental policy in 1972'.[261] And from an economic approach, Professor Winter distinguished, in 1989, four phases 'in the relationship between man and his life conditions'.[262] Even more, mentioned evolution shows that

260. Laura van der Meer, *Environmental Liability Regimes: Approaches and Best Practices* (Belgium: International Environmental Resources, 2006), 6–8. Mentioned author concludes 'with suggestions for step-wise approach to liability for countries considering liability and redress with respect to LMOs'. It is part of the Compilation of Expert Papers concerning Liability and Redress and Living Modified Organisms (2nd edn., January 2006) published by CropLife International regarding the Cartagena Protocol on Biosafety. It is possible to download the complete Compilation of Expert Papers at the following web site address: www.croplife.org/library/documents/ Biotech%20issues/ BSP%20page/2004_02_%2026_PUB_Independant%20Handbook%20Liability%20and%20Redress_ 2E.pdf (accessed 24 Jan. 2010).

261. Neil Gunningham, *Environmental Law, Regulation and Governance: Shifting Architectures* 21 J. Envtl. L. 179–212 (2009).

262. Prof. Gerd Winter, *Perspectives for Environmental Law, Entering the Fourth Phase* (Oxford U. Press, 1989). Downloaded from the J. Envtl. L. on 7 Jul. 2011.

Eleftheriadis is right when arguing that 'environmental duties cannot easily be turned into rights'.[263]

389. In Latin America, a survey of recent developments in environmental regulation suggests:

> the following general trends: (1) new or amended constitutions often include environmental principles; (2) economic legislation that incorporates environmental requirements; (3) more comprehensive and systematic environmental regulations; (4) decentralized environmental legislative authority; (5) structural legal changes making it easier to promulgate environmental laws; (6) an increase in regional, bilateral and international environmental laws; and (7) a strengthening of state custodianship over certain environmental interests.[264]

390. In this Part IV, we will present the characteristics of the environmental liability regime in Argentina. As it will be seen, several kinds of liabilities may arise in cases of environmental damages or when there is a breach of an environmental law or permit. They emerge from the General Environmental Law 25675 of 2002, the administrative liability, the civil and the criminal liabilities. The whole environmental liability system is related to the Argentine Civil Code and particularly to the specific rules set forth by Law 25675 of 2002 (the General Law on the Environment), and Law 24051 of 1992 on Hazardous Waste. Criminal and Administrative liability provisions will also be presented according to the crimes ruled by the Argentine Penal Code and the Hazardous Waste Law 24051 of 1992.

391. The rules and principles that govern civil liability will be discussed in Chapter 2. We will focus on the rules emerging from criminal liability in Chapter 3. Because of its relevance, current developments on mandatory environmental insurance will be also referred in Chapter 2.

---

263. Pavlos Eleftheriadis, *Environmental Rights in the EC Legal Order* (University of Oxford Faculty of Law Legal Studies Research Paper Series, Working Paper No. 24/2007, Sep. 2007), 1. As mentioned author points out environmental duties are imperfect in the sense that they are not owed to identifiable individuals. Even when we can specify in great detail and with great clarity the duties imposed by environmental standards, we cannot always transform such standards into easily identifiable rights. Because such standards are meant to protect and entitle either future generations or the countless fellow human beings who share the world with us, the presumed beneficiaries or holders of such rights are unable or unlikely to claim the correlative duties through actions of their own. The full text may be downloaded from the Social Science Research Network electronic library at: http://ssrn.com/abstract=1015923 (accessed 29 Oct. 2010).

264. Juan Carlos Urquidi Fell, *Environmental Issues in Commercial Transactions Involving Companies Doing Business in Latin America.* (s/d s/l).

Chapter 2. Civil Liability

§1. INTRODUCTION

392. By the time the author is writing this book, a bill drafted by the National Executive Power is being discussed in the National Congress regarding the unification of the Civil and Commercial Codes in the country. The environmental aspects of said bill are analysed by Valls in his work "*Proyecto de Ley de Reforma, Actualización y Unificación de los Códigos Civil y Comercial. Regulación del ambiente y de los derechos de incidencia colectiva*" [Bill for the Reform, Update and Unification of the Civil and Comercial Codes. Regulation of the Environment and the Collective Incidente Rights]

In October 2014, the new Civil and Commercial Code was passed through Law 26994 (published in the Official Gazette on 8 October 2014). This Code unifies the existing Civil and Commercial Codes and will come into force in 1 January 2016. From an environmental standpoint, the basic parameters on civil liability are maintained and are joined with those parameters set forth under Law 25675, sections 27–34. However, for certain part of the doctrine, although section 1716 of the new code sets forth the duty to repair the damage caused, it has a different provision on the duty to repair the environment, duty that is considered a priority under section 41 of the National Constitution. Speaking about damages, section 1737 of the new code states that '*there is damage when a right or interest related to a person, to an estate or to a collective right not condemned by the legal system is affected*'.

393. The legal regime set forth by the Argentine Civil Code[265] establishes liability for negligence and also provides for strict liability depending on the cases: liability for negligence is applicable mainly to the breach of contractual obligations according to the provisions set forth by Articles 1109 and 512 of the Argentine Civil Code,[266] while strict liability emerges in the extra-contractual obligations field according to Article 1113 of the same legal body.

265. The Argentine Civil Code was approved by Law 340 of 1869. It was intended to be amended in 1926 (draft elaborated by Dr Juan Bibiloni) in 1936, 1954 and 1987, in 1993 and in 1998. Regarding the liability regime, the unification in the field of contractual and non-contractual liability is ruled by all mentioned Draft Civil Codes by unifying both contractual and non-contractual liability systems. For a complete study on it see Luis F.P. Leiva Fernandez, *The Civil Code of the Republic of Argentina: Its Past, Its Present and Its Future*. In the net: www.leivafernandez.com.ar/ The_civil_code_arg_china.pdf (accessed 23 Feb. 2010).

266. Article 1109 reads 'Any person performing an act which through his fault of negligence causes damage to another, is obliged to repair the damage. This obligation is governed by the same provisions to which the offenses of the civil law are subject.' Art. 512 reads: 'The debtor's negligence in the fulfillment of an obligation consist in the omission of those measures which the nature of the obligation calls for, and which correspond to the circumstances of persons, of time and of place.'

That is why fault-based liability arises as the general liability rule when it is claimed on the basis of an existing contract or a previous juridical *liaison* between a plaintiff and a defendant.[267]

394. Regarding civil liability for environmental damage, we will see that specific rules in Argentine are set forth by the General Law on the Environment 25675 of 2002. Articles 27–33 of the aforementioned legal body govern the 'environmental damage of collective incidence' by structuring a regime based on strict liability premises.[268] Law 25675 of 2002 is not the only rule governing civil liability in cases of environmental damage, as other Argentine environmental norms are applicable, for instance, to industrial waste management.

They are set forth by Law 25612 of 2002, which provides not only a civil liability regime but also an administrative liability regime for industrial and services waste management. Moreover, it has to be noted that the original text of Law 25612 of 2002 contained provisions on criminal liability for damages related to industrial waste management but they were vetoed by the national Executive Power (when said Law was promulgated) on the grounds that they overlapped with the criminal provisions of the Hazardous Waste Law 24051 of 1992.

395. This complex legal liability scheme will be approached in this work. According to its particular regulation in Law 25675 of 2002, civil liability for environmental collective damage will be dealt with in §2 III of this chapter.

We will discuss the substantive legislation in this Part IV.

396. The way in which these rights can be enforced in court will be analysed in Part V of this work.

The legislation, case law and legal doctrine in this Part have been, as much as possible, updated until November 2011.

§2. Liability for Negligence

397. Let us make clear that liability based on negligence is not applicable to the compensation of environmental damages of collective incidence in Argentina because in those cases strict liability is mandatory, according to Article 28 of Law 25675 of 2002. The abovementioned Article states that anyone who causes environmental damage will be strictly responsible for the re-establishment of the conditions precedent to the damage. Should it be not technically feasible, the substitutive

267. The Argentine private-law system is based on the civil or continental law, because the Argentine Civil Code is based on the French Civil Code approved in 1804. This may also be seen in most Latin American private-law codes which follow the principles and general structure of the Napoleon Code from 1804.

268. Even before Law 25675 was passed in 2002, authors had written that the amendment of the Argentine National Constitution from 1994 which introduced environmental rules and principles in Art. 41 seemed to have been inspired in the strict liability system set forth by the Locarno Convention of 1991. See Jorge Mosset Iturraspe et al., *Daño Ambiental* (Buenos Aires: Rubinzal Culzoni, 1999), 1:240.

compensation to be determined by justice shall be transferred to the Environmental Compensation Fund created by said Law (but not implemented yet) which will be administered by the enforcement Authority (the SAyDS). This is without prejudice of other legal actions that may be applicable to the case.

398. Furthermore, and in order to present a general feature of this subject matter, it must be noted that the basis of liability for negligence in the Argentine civil legal system are Articles 512 and 1109 of the Civil Code[269] which establish general rules for negligence or fault. A person is at fault when he acts 'contrary to the rules of prudence generally accepted in a given society at a particular time and place'.[270] Article 1109 of the Argentine Civil Code provides that anyone who performs an

Next Page is Argentina – 127

269. Félix Trigo Represas & Marcelo López Mesa, *Tratado de la Responsabilidad Civil* (Buenos Aires: La Ley, 2004), 1:53.
270. See *Liability for one's own acts*, Argentine Civil Code, 14 in http://books.google.com.ar/books?id=EKoPfh4UuPAC&pg=RA1-PA8&lpg=RA1-A8&dq=art+1113+argentine+civil+code&source=bl&ots=JsfxMzO21D&sig=2G5cie3b_Vxt90-PWhlIH6lI8nQ&hl=es&ei=vuRXTfKPDYGCtge5md2hDQ&sa=X&oi=book_result&ct=result&resnum=5&ved=0CDEQ6AEwBA#v=onepage&q=art%201113%20argentine%20civil%20code&f=false.

action through which his fault or negligence causes damage to another is bound to compensate his harm. The legal doctrine agrees[271] that three are the conditions to be demonstrated in order to obtain compensation based on Article 1109: fault, damage and a causal relationship between the two precedent conditions. The three conditions are required to be liable for damages caused by both positive actions and omissions.

I. Fault

399. There basically are two levels of fault or negligence in Argentina according to its classical roman-law origins, one being the 'general' concept of fault and the other, the 'specific' concept. The general concept comprises both simple fault and wilful misconduct. Simple fault exists when somebody's conduct is imprudent, negligent or he acts without due knowledge of what he has to perform properly. In contrast, intentional fault is committed with wilful misconduct[272] when a person causes damage with the intention to do so. It must be noted that gross negligence is an intermediate concept between the simple negligence and the intentional fault, and despite not being defined by the Argentine Civil Code, it is usually included in insurance contracts as a cause of insurer's exemption of liability.

400. The fault on the performance of an obligation consists in the omission of the procedures that the nature of the obligation itself demands and that correspond to the circumstances of people, time and place.[273] Out of the contractual obligations area, that is, in the field of tort law, the fault as a civil liability attributive factor is provided by Articles 1109 and 1113, second paragraph, first part of the Civil Code. Article 1109 provides that every person who performs an action and due to his fault or negligence inflicts damage to another person he is obliged to compensate for the damage.

401. Doctrine, when refers to the environmental care, meant that more than an individual right it is a social right. The social importance of environment prevails over the individual prerogative pertaining to it:

> The activity in this regard must be decisively oriented under a solidarism perspective (which considers law as a social event; that exists "by" man, "with" man and "for" man, according to Bidart Campos, and articulating man with society. And that leads us to think of the repair obligation not only as a consequence of an offense liability but as a result of social solidarity. (Principle: whoever enjoys *commodum* must suffer the correlative *periculum*). Thus, liability makes evident the impact of what we call solidarism. In the same way, the admission of the right abuse in our civil system leads us to one of the most

271. Jorge Joaquín Llambías, *Tratado de Derecho Civil, Parte General* (Buenos Aires: Abeledo Perrot, 1978), 1:75.
272. Wilful misconduct refers to actions committed with intention to cause harm.
273. Such is the definition of 'fault' established by Art. 512 of the Argentine Civil Code.

fruitful applications established through Article 2618 of the Civil Code: the regular use of the property. This regulation, inspired by Articles 844 of the Italian Civil Code, 906 of the German Code, and 684 of the Swiss Code, regulates the nuisances that exceed what is reasonable and those which are unbearable. In such a case, the nuisance should be eliminated or lessened independently from the neighbour's fault. The judge is highly empowered to order the cessation and even bring such unpleasant activity to an end. The judge can also establish the measures to be taken in the sentence. The criteria of the requirements of production and use priority are not independent but complementary, being able to execute the elimination even though the neighbour is settled near the place of the nuisance when it already existed.[274]

402. At the other end of liability based upon the generic notion of fault, there exits wilful misconduct, which consists of the intention to damage, and it could be direct or incidental wilful misconduct.

403. In an intermediate level, between the notions of fault and wilful misconduct, there exists *gross negligence* as provided by Article 70 of the Insurance Law 17418 of 1967 and functions as the cause for exoneration of the insurer's liability. This kind of fault lacks a legal definition and its content has resulted from jurisprudence evolution.

404. The concept of 'gross negligence' is closely connected to environmental liability. There is a model of insurance policy approved by the National Superintendent of Insurance Companies to cover environmental damages.

II. Damage

405. As Laurent Proot and Hubert Bocken (Ghent University, Belgium) express:

> [t]he notions "environmental damage" and "ecological damage" (impairment of nature) are especially used in the European law order. In the US, the notion "damage to natural resources" is used. Natural resources are among others land, fish, wild animals, air, water, drinking water resources which are owned or governed by the US, a state, a local authority, a foreign authority or an Indian tribe. No distinction is made between appropriated and not appropriated goods.[275]

274. In *re 'CO.DE.CI de la Provincia de Río Negro s Amparo Ambiental'*, Sentence by the Supreme Tribunal of the Province of Río Negro of 16 Aug. 2005 published by www.eldial.com.ar AX21AA (accessed 29 Mar. 2010).

275. Before studying the rules regarding damage to the marine environment Proot and Bocken point out that 'the notion of "environmental damage" has to be clearly defined'. Mr Laurent Proot & Prof. Dr Hubert Bocken (Centre for Environmental Law – Ghent University, Belgium) '*Environmental Damage and Belgian Law*' in *Marine Resource Damage Assessment, Liability and Compensation for Environmental Damage* 27–29 (Springer 2005). Mentioned authors also refer to the notions of

406. In Argentina, there are no differences in the legal consequences between ecological damage, environmental damage and environmental pollution. Even though the doctrine generally refers to 'environmental pollution' when dealing with crimes sanctioned by the Hazardous Waste Law 24051 of 1992, and to 'environmental damage' when dealing with civil liability for environmental damages. The jurisprudence has stated that not all damage to nature comprises an unlawful damage, being it necessary to reconcile the environment protection with other goods equally valuable for the community.[276]

407. It must be noted that different kinds of damages are ruled by the Argentine legal system: direct damages, indirect damages (which include loss of chance) and moral damages.

408. Specifically, environmental damage is determined by four normative orders which are applied according to the damage inflicted: related to vicinity relations (Article 2618 of the Civil Code), or caused by the risk or vice of the object (Article 1113, second paragraph, second part of the Civil Code), or when it is an environmental collective damage (Law 25675 of 2002); or when it is related to industrial wastes (Law 25612 of 2002). The specifications of each of these assumptions will be analysed below.

409. The environmental damage regarding vicinity relations is the one caused by non-material propagation or nuisance that exceeds the 'normal tolerance' and comes from near buildings extending past the boundaries of the property. In said assumptions, legal protection works even when the causes for the environmental damage have an administrative authorization according to the Article 2618 of the Civil Code, anticipating that the interference with the quiet enjoyment originated from smoke, heat, smells, brightness, noises, vibrations or similar damage due to the activities in neighbouring property do not exceed the normal tolerance, taking into account the conditions of the place, and even if there exits due authorization. In accordance with the circumstances of the cases, the judges may provide the compensation of damage or the cessation of such interferences.

410. In the implementation of these norms, the judges should examine the requirements of the property according to its main use and bear in mind the 'priority of use' principle.[277]

'ecological damage', 'pure ecological damage' and 'impairment of the nature'. And 'for a comprehensive review of the importance of the definition of the notion 'environmental damage' they recommend the reading of Brans E.H.P. (2001), *Liability for damage to public natural resources. Standing, damage and damage assessment* 9 (The Hague/London/New York, Kluwer Law International).

276. This is the doctrine of the sentence in re *Louzán Carlos v. Ministerio de Economía s Acción de Amparo*, rendered by Room I of the Federal Chamber of Appeals of San Martín, dated as of 26 Jul. 1993 and published by La Ley 1995, E, 375 et seq.

277. Due to obvious reasons, the Code does not either define the concept of 'vicinity' nor set a distance to which the operational capacity of the legal precept should adjust, establishing, with good criterion that in order to apply this norm, there should be taken into account 'the conditions of the

411. The second normative plexus of environmental damage is subjected to liability for the risk or vice of the object, that is, strict liability. As it will be seen later in §3 I of this chapter, the environmental damage triggered 'by' risk or vice of the object has a different legal doctrine than the damage triggered 'with' the object. Such difference does not relate to legal consequences but to the liability exemption of the person who caused damage. In effect, if the environmental damage is triggered by the object, the origin of the damage is the person who makes use of it as an instrument.

412. However, if the environmental damage is caused by risk or vice of the object, it is the object (by itself faulty or dangerous) which originated the damage and the owner or guardian of it is held liable for the damage caused. We will refer to those paragraphs later on.

413. The third nominative order relates to environmental collective damage. The General Law of the Environment, 25675 of 2002, introduces the specific legal concept of 'environmental collective damage' in Argentina, which is closely connected to the provisions set forth by Article 41 of the NC.

414. The main rules on environmental collective damage are set forth by Articles 27–33 of Law 25675 of 2002. These articles, together with Article 22 of Law 25675 of 2002 (according to which environmental insurance is mandatory in the country) are considered as statutory federal law by the Argentine legal doctrine. That is why the provinces and local counties are not entitled to regulate over these matters, having only capacity to approve 'procedural' or 'administrative' rules related to them.[278]

415. Article 27 of Law 25675 of 2002 specifically defines environmental damage as 'every relevant alteration which negatively modifies the environment, its resources, the balance of the ecosystems, or the collective goods or values'. It is a broad definition that includes harm not only to the environment considered as a whole, but also to any of its resources (air, water, soil, fauna, flora); and even more, it comprises harm which adversely affects the collective goods and/or values.

416. Having said that, one may conclude that the main features environmental damage according to Law 25675 of 2002 are as follows: (i) it may be equally referred to as 'environmental damage' or as 'environmental *collective* damage'; (ii) it is legally defined as 'any relevant alteration which causes a negative modification

---

place'. This is the current text of Art. 2618, after it was amended in 1968 by Law 17711 of 1968 which – besides- derogated Art. 2619. Before said amendment, environmental damages linked to vicinity were set forth by Arts 2618 and 2619 of the Civil Code and the doctrine (Guillermo Borda, *Tratado de Derecho Civil*, Part IV, t I 398) criticized the limited field of the legal protection and its operational capacity (only noise and industrial facilities damages were examined) and due to the fact that these articles did not establish the authority judges nowadays have to order the cessation of interference (they only could pass fines).

278. Daniel A. Sabsay y María E. Di Paola, *El Daño Ambiental Colectivo y la Ley General del Ambiente* (Buenos Aires: La Ley. Anales de Legislación Argentina, Boletín Informativo, 2003), 17: 1–9.

of the environment, its resources, the ecosystems' balance or the collective goods and values'; (iii) it is governed by a regime of strict liability; (iv) the first obligation that arises in cases of environmental damage is to 'restore [the environment] to the precedent condition',[279] (v) if mentioned restoration is not technically possible, a compensation for damages must be determined by courts and transferred to the Environmental Compensation Fund (created by Article 34 of Law 25675 of 2002 which is based on the idea of the *Superfund* created by CERCLA in the USA, but not implemented yet in Argentina), without prejudice of other judicial actions that may be filed, and (vi) it is possible to be exempted from environmental liability only when: (a) it is demonstrated that damage occurred notwithstanding the person who caused it has taken all appropriate measures to avoid it, or (b) if it is demonstrated that damage exists because of the exclusive fault of the victim or of the third party's action or omission.

417. Relevant cases as *Copetro* and *Municipalidad de Tandil* are related to environmental collective damage, in particular, the latter, in which the Supreme Court of the Province of Buenos Aires sustained a claim for compensation for environmental damage apart from damage inflicted to people.

418. The fourth nominative order is related to environmental damage due to the usage of industrial wastes, which is provided by Law 25612 of 2002.

419. Regarding the amount of compensations for environmental damages, it should be mentioned that there are no monetary limits established by law. Even though it may seem reasonable, some problems have recently arise in Argentina, particularly because of the fact that environmental insurance is mandatory, as it was previously seen in Part IV, Chapter 2 §4 of this work.[280]

III. Causation

420. The Argentine legal doctrine and jurisprudence unanimously consider causation as an unavoidable requisite for liability both in the contractual and the noncontractual (liability in tort) fields. Legal doctrine on causation is rich and authors -particularly those who write on civil and criminal law subjects- have developed the particular features of mentioned requisite in connection with the different kind of liabilities. The Hon. civil Judge Llambías was one of the most authoritative Argentine civil writers who best explained what causation is from a legal point of view (or, in other words, what make causation relevant for legal consideration) and how it differs from its approach from the physical sciences' point of view.[281]

279. According to what is ruled by Art. 41 of the national Constitution.
280. For further developments, please see §4 of this chapter.
281. According to his opinion, juridical causation emerges when the 'nexus of material causation is adjusted or corrected following to the prism of justice'. Jorge Joaquín Llambías, *Los distintos tipos de causalidad jurídicamente relevantes*, en Estudios en Homenaje a Héctor Lafaille. Bs. As. Depalma, 1968, 452.

421. Different theories have been developed regarding the scope and relevance of causation relationships. In essence, they seek answer 'to the following question: when is a result referable to the voluntary performance of a person?'[282] We will mention in general to those theories that have impact on judicial decisions: the doctrine of 'the equivalent conditions', the theory for which the 'nearest cause' prevails, the doctrine of the 'most efficient cause' and the doctrine of the 'adequate causation' which is the most followed by the Argentine courts.

422. As it is well known, Maximilian von Buri developed the theory of the equivalent conditions (*conditio sine qua non*) according to which 'cause' is any precedent condition which added to the other existing ones produce a result or, reversely, any precedent condition without which the result would not exist as such. The 'nearest cause' theory emphasizes the relevance of the latter cause or the last condition that occurred or took place in the moment previous (or in the 'nearest moment') to the result. The theory of the most 'efficient' cause considers 'cause' only that relevant precedent condition which even though if isolated from the other ones leads to a factual result. Finally, the 'adequate causation theory' concludes that 'cause' is only the precedent condition which, according to the natural and ordinary course of things, carries or leads regularly to a given result. In other words, this theory considers relevant what ordinarily and naturally results under similar conditions.

423. The Argentine Civil Code adopted the theory of the adequate causation and prevision is essential to determine causation, according to Article 901 of mentioned legal body.

§3. Strict Liability

I. Strict Liability in the Civil Code

424. Strict liability was not established in the original version of Argentine Civil Code. It was introduced when it was amended by Law 17711 in 1968, through the addition of two paragraphs to the original Article 1113 of the Argentine Civil Code. Those second and third paragraphs added to Article 1113 became the cornerstone of the Argentine strict liability regime for damages arising from the inherent 'risk or vice of the object'. To claim compensation based on strict liability rules the 'victim' is released to prove fault or negligence by the tortfeasor and it is mandatory for him only to render proof of the damage suffered and of the causal relationship between damage and the defendant's conduct.

425. The exoneration doctrine of liability by Article 1113 of the Civil Code states a difference related to the harm inflicted 'with' the object or 'by' the risk or vice of the object.

---

282. Sebastian Soler, *Derecho Penal Argentino* (Buenos Aires: Tipográfica Editora Argentina, 1999), 2:354.

426. If the damage was caused 'with' the object, in order to be exonerated of liability, the owner of the object or whomever the guardian might be, must prove that it was not his fault. However, if the damage was inflicted 'by' risk or vice of the object in order to be exonerated of liability the owner or guardian is not entitled to prove its lack of fault but the victim's or third party's fault.[283]

II. Strict Liability in Treaties

427. Strict liability is the general rule in cases related to damages caused by hazardous waste and nuclear damage, as expressly stated by the laws and regulations that govern mentioned activities.

428. As it was expressed in paragraph 66 of this work, Argentina is a Party of the main international environmental treaties so their rules are applicable to the country, unless otherwise expressed at the time of ratifying or accession to them.[284]

III. Liability Related to Industrial and Hazardous Waste

429. Several approaches of liability arising from the management of industrial waste and wastes produced by service activities are defined by Title II of Law 25612 of 2002.[285] Thus, 'civil liability' and 'administrative liability' are structured by Chapters I and II of mentioned law, from Articles 40–50. Criminal liability was included in the original version of this Law, but Decree 1313 of 2002 promulgated Law 25612 and deleted the criminal liability rules. That is why criminal liabilities

---

283. As Rychlak and Case sharply define it, 'strict liability is a legal doctrine that makes some persons responsible for damages their actions or products cause, regardless of any "fault" on their part'. Ronald J. Rychlak & David W. Case *Environmental Law* 22 (Oceana-Oxford U. Press, 2010). Art. 1113 of the original version of the Argentine Civil Code established a presumption of fault, against the owner of the things. Mentioned original Article consisted of only one paragraph (which is still effective) and reads: 'The obligation of a person who has caused damage extends to the damages caused by the persons who depend upon him, or by the things of which he makes use or which he has under his care.' In 1968 Law 17711 added the following paragraphs to this Article: 'If damage was caused with the objects, their owner or guardian has to prove that there was no fault from his part in order to be exempt from liability; but if damage was caused by the risk or vice of the object he will only be exempt from liability totally or in part if he proves fault from the victim or from a third party for whom he is not obliged to response.' (Second paragraph). 'Should the object be used against the express or presumed will of its owner or guardian, he will not be liable.' (Third paragraph).

284. Regarding the enforcement of transnational civil liability claims before municipal courts, it is interesting to learn from Professor Churchill's article when he examines 'the progress that has so far been made in concluding treaties to facilitate the bringing of civil liability claims for compensation before municipal courts' and considers 'how such treaties have operated in practice, and […] what lessons may be learned from them, particularly in regard to the feasibility and desirability of concluding further treaties, as called for by Principle 13 of the Rio Declaration'. Prof. Robin R. Churchill, *Facilitating (Transnational) Civil Liability Litigation for Environmental Damage by Means of Treaties: Problems, Progress and Prospects,* 12 Y.B. Intl. Envtl. L. 3–41 (2001). See http://yielaw.oxfordjournals.org. Downloaded on 28 Feb. 2011.

285. This law governs the Management of Industrial and Service's Activities Wastes.

related to industrial and service activities wastes are governed by Law 24051 of 1992 on Hazardous Waste.

430. Regarding the management of industrial waste it must be said that each of these wastes as defined by Article 2 of Law 25612 of 2002 is presumed[286] to be a 'risky thing' as defined by the second paragraph of Article 1113 of the Argentine Civil Code. So liability in these cases is strict.

431. Even more, the fact of having abandoned, sold or passed title of aforementioned industrial waste cannot be argued as a defence if liability is claimed.

432. Furthermore, the owner or guardian of the waste is not exempted from liability in cases where fault was committed by a third party if damage could have been avoided by adopting the due care according the particular circumstances that surround each case.

433. Particularly in the province of Buenos Aires, Law 14343 of 2012 was recently passed (BOPBA dated as of 23 January 2012)[287] and regulates the identification of environmental liabilities and establishes the obligation to repair the polluted sites in that province.

§4. Environmental Insurance

I. General Principles

434. When it there exists hazardous activities for the environment, a special environmental insurance is compulsory according to Article 22 of Law 25675 of 2002. In accordance with this norm, any individual or legal entity, public or private, who engages in risky activities for the environment, the ecosystems or its constitutive elements, shall hire an insurance policy to guarantee his liability for damages to the environment that could be inflicted. Likewise, and depending upon the case and possibilities, he could join an environmental restoration fund which would enable restoration measures to be implemented. Said insurance is fully operative and the SAyDS has passed specific norms establishing minimum insurance amounts and even adopting an insurance policy model to cover such risks, as we will see later.

435. At the time, when no administrative regulations regarding environment insurance existed, in the Supreme Court the fact of hiring or not such insurance was debated. In cases such as *Asociación de Superficiarios de la Patagonia v. YPF*, the

286. This is a *juris tantum* presumption established by Art. 40 of Law 25612 of 2002 is applicable to the Management of Industrial and Service' Activities Wastes.

287. Comments on the Environmental Liabilities Law of the Province of Buenos Aires by Martín Alejo Prieto, at www.eldial.com supplement: Doctrine dated 7 May 2012.

Supreme Court decided that such lack of regulations did not prevent Article 22 from coming into effect.[288]

436. Environmental insurance is a management tool not unanimously accepted by the Argentine doctrine.[289] However, Law 25675 of 2002 on Environment sets forth that they are mandatory. The law's regulation adapted its scope and practical application to certain conditions on a case-by-case basis, according to the Environmental Complexity Level (ECL).

In a recent decision dated 11 December 2014, the Supreme Court of Justice restored the validity of the mandatory environmental insurance in Argentina. As it was already mentioned, such insurance is ruled by section 22 of the Environmental Law No. 25675 as regulated by the standards issued by the Secretary of Environment and Sustainable Development and the Superintendency of Insurance. The insurance can be taken out by means of a collective environmental damage bond or liability insurance policy according to the Executive Order No. 1638/12 and Resolution No. 37160 of the Superintendency of Insurance.

However, the Federal Court in Administrative matters No. 9 of the City of Buenos Aires had cancelled the enforcement of said insurance when, in 26 December 2012, it issued its ruling in *re 'Fundación Medio Ambiente v. Estado Nacional Poder Ejecutivo Nacional*, Decreto N° 1638/12 – Resolución N° 37160 de la Superintendencia de Seguros de la Nación s/ Medida Cautelar Autónoma'. Said ruling was appealed by the National Government but the Court of Appeals in Administrative matters of the City of Buenos Aires confirmed the ruling of the Federal Court in First Instance No. 9.

The National Government filed an appeal with the Supreme Court of Justice and on 11 December 2014, the Supreme Court in consistency with the Attorney General Office's decision contested judgment and restored the enforcement of the standards that request a collective environmental insurance. The Supreme Court of Justice argued that the Court of Appeals did not consider the environmental constitutional grounds, did not consider the principle of environmental responsibility and paralysed the Government's environmental policy. In practice, the file will be referred back to the Federal Court of Appeals in Administrative matters for the latter to issue a new ruling considering the Supreme Court of Justice's decision.

---

288. See the comments by Dr Mariana Valls de Rossi untitled, *El daño Ambiental en la Corte Suprema Argentina. Recomposición. Obligación de contratar un seguro.* They are related to the case *Asociación de Superficiarios de la Patagonia c YPF SA s Daño Ambiental*, sentenced by the Supreme Court of Justice on 13 Jul. 2004. Published in www.prodiversitas.bioetica.org/des59.htm (accessed 12 Sep. 2011).
289. Professor Pigretti, for example, disagrees. In one of his books he states that 'Capitalism should defend the environment as a survival goal' and also states that Pope John Paul II talked about 'wild capitalism'; two words 'that are sufficient to identify the problem'. He also confirms, among other concepts, that 'the lack of humanism disallows and destroys the advantages attributed to globalization'. He concludes that 'laws suggesting a strict commercial compensation regime are usually passed. Insurance policies that do not provide a positive outcome across the world, bank guarantees that are never sufficient, trust funds profitable for their trustors and other formulae such as the economic limits on compensations are ridiculous when it is necessary to restore the environment'. Eduardo A. Pigretti, *Derecho Ambiental Profundizado* (Buenos Aires: La Ley, 2004), 2–4.

437. So as to provide the interpreter with guiding technical steps referring to the specific norms on environmental damage in Argentina, the so-called *Unidad de Evaluación de Riesgos Ambientales* of the SAyDS (UERA as per its acronym in Spanish) in 2008 drafted a report about technical considerations related to the environmental damage cover. This report tries to:

> give a practical interpretation from scientific knowledge to environmental damage concept according to the regulation drafted by the National Environmental Authority to make Articles 22, 27 and 28 of the General Law of Environment enter into force. It should not be forgotten in such an attempt that the final result must have the characteristic of being viable in practical terms, facilitating stages where it could be possible, but without neglecting the comprehensive point of view of the completeness which characterizes such definition.[290]

438. The environmental insurance regulation in Argentina provides a series of particular rules with a list of the items and service activities whose ECL has to be determined based on a polynomial formula approved by the Unit of Environmental Risks Assessments (UERA as per its acronym in Spanish). The ECLs are three: low, average and high and the duty to take out environmental insurance policies is applicable for average and high levels. The regulation issued by the SAyDS also provides Basic Guidelines for the Contractual Conditions of Environmental Collective Responsibility Insurance Policies (they are bonds offered by authorized companies and provide insurance based on a standard insurance policy that has been approved by the National Insurance Superintendence).

439. To financially guarantee environmental compensation, insurance companies usually ask for a risk rating report, copy of the last three balance sheets, copy of the bylaws, an affidavit for the company's rating (additional questions), sureties (or other types of liability insurances) and an asset statement.

440. In Argentina, the environmental insurance policy contains three interested parties: the insurer (who covers the risks and obliges to provide remedy or indemnity), the policyholder (responsible for the contamination and is the one who hires the insurance) and the insured or beneficiary (the national, provincial or municipal state or the city of Buenos Aires and the ACUMAR).

441. The norm entrusted the UERA of the SAyDS with determining the proper risky activities among other functions of organizational and technical character.

442. In the Argentine market, there exist insurance companies that cover the environmental damage risk of collective incidence. The hiring conditions vary according to the cases, but the insurance policy is always the same one since it is related to the approved model for such purposes.

---

290. Miguel Mateu, *Configuración y Recomposición del Daño Ambiental* (Buenos Aires: Documento de Trabajo, UERA SAyDS, Nov. 2008).

443. It is related to specific coverage insurance: that of 'environmental damage of collective incidence'. It is considered as such, that damage that implies a relevant and negative alteration of the environment or its resources because it constitutes: (a) an unacceptable risk for human health or; (b) the destruction of a natural resource or the deterioration that limits its self-generating capacity. It is not pointless to remember that this coverage must allow the facing of the remedy operations with promptness by which it should be independent and alien of any other responsibility either criminal civil or administrative.

444. Regarding the Minimum Insurance Amount of Sufficient Entity, according to the norm in force adopted by Resolution 481 of 2011 of SAyDS, it is applicable to every fixed industrial activity facility and that of similar or higher complexity services than the ECL 14,5 after the compliance of the adjustment of section A.1.2 of Appendix II of Resolution 177 of 2007 issued by SAyDS, and its modified resolutions.[291]

445. With national Decree 1638 of 2012, the regime regarding environmental insurance was modified, since said regulation, as Silva Garretón goes, permits "hiring two types of insurance": (a) Surety Insurance on Environmental Damage of Collective Incidence, which already existed in the market and (b) Liability Insurance on Environmental Damage of Collective Incidence. As this author wisely says, Article 5 of the Decree sets forth that the insurable minimum amount (MMA in Spanish) of the suitable entity will be set by the insurance company, which will be supported by the suitable entity regarding the coverage required by Article 22 of Law 25675 and that the entity should make an assessment of the Initial Environmental Situation (SAI in Spanish) so as to report on risks and detect pre-existing damage, keeping the documentation for a ten-year period. However, on 17 October 2012, "the Superintendent's Office of National Insurance passed Resolution 37160 through which approves the general conditions in a general and standardized way for both the "Compulsory Security Insurance on Environmental Damage of Collective Incidence" and "Compulsory Insurance of Liability on Environmental Damage of Collective Incidence" and modifies item 23.6 of the Insurance Activity Rulebook incorporating as a subject matter the coverage of Environmental Damage of Collective Incidence in which only general approvals can be applied.

446. Specifically and regarding the normative application of environmental insurances to port activities, the author of this monograph has elaborated a special work for the Argentine Port Council in August 2009 titled 'Report on the Legal Regime of Environmental Insurances and its Impact in Ports' analysing the scope of a unique issue that back then was in its full evolution.[292]

---

291. At the same time, the basic guidelines for the contractual conditions of the environmental damage of collective incidence insurance policy are set by the joint Resolution 1973 of 2007 by SAyDS and Resolution 98 of 2007 of the Secretariat of Finances of the Department of Economy and Production.

292. Access to the complete text is available at www.consejoportuario.com.ar/informes.aspx and www.estudiovillano.com (accessed 2 Nov. 2011).

II. Rules for the Matanza-Riachuelo Basin

447. The obligation to hire environmental insurances for companies developing their activities in the Matanza-Riachuelo Basin is ruled by Resolution 34 of 2010 passed by the Authority of the Matanza-Riachuelo Basin (ACUMAR). This norm states the admissibility requirements for the Industrial Restructuring Programme in said basin and states that an insurance policy 'in favour of ACUMAR must be presented'.[293]

448. At the same time, in the legal reasons of the Resolution 34 of 2010 ACUMAR, there is focus on the obligation established by Article 22 of Law 25675 of 2002 which constitutes a requirement to be fulfilled by generators, transporters and operators of hazardous waste who ask for the annual environmental certificate and for any other risky activity in which industrial and/or hazardous waste are handled.

449. Said regulation states that every service industry or institution that is declared as Contaminating Agent by the ACUMAR must hire an environmental insurance established by Article 22 of Law 25675 of 2002 and its complementary regulation.

450. In this very complex judicial case on 20 December 2012, and aiming at channelling the execution process of the sentence dated as of 08 July 2008, the National Supreme Court of Justice passed a resolution that provided Federal Judge of Quilmes to be dismissed. It distributed the responsibility in the following way: the National Judge on Criminal and Correctional Matters No. 12 is now in charge of "temporarily controlling contracts signed or to be signed within the drinking water and sewer supply plan" while "all the remaining competences stated by the sentence of 08 July 08 dealing with the high, medium and low basin of the Matanza Riachuelo rivers" are temporarily assigned to the Federal Judge on Criminal and Correctional Matters No. 2 of Morón, province of Buenos Aires.

Due to this division of competences and bearing in mind the "broad territory area covered by the basin and also the various and complex aspects that should be taken into account", the National Supreme Court of Justice ordered the new judges to place special emphasis on the following topics: the relocation of industrial premises, measurement systems for air and water quality, the detection of clandestine connections, the eradication and relocation of poor neighbourhoods near the Sewage Treatment Plant of the Berazategui's Bicentenary Plant of Dock Sud (in the province of Buenos Aires), the environmental epidemiology control system, the health services network and the industrial restructuring plan of the Basin.

293. Article 1 of Resolution 34 of ACUMAR with the introduced modifications by Resolution 163 of 2011 of ACUMAR. It is worth noting that for such objectives to be fulfilled, ACUMAR must be the 'insured' or 'beneficiary' in the respective insurance policy.

Chapter 3. Criminal Liability

§1. Introduction

451. The Argentine Penal Code does not expressly set forth crimes already determined to protect *'the environment'* as such and in a direct way. That is why there is no environmental criminal law in Argentina, yet. However, we should clear out that this does not mean that there are no crimes applicable indirectly to judge the criminal liability for pollution as damage crimes may be[294] and among those which protect the security and public health (which are the most suitable to guard our environment today) those are: the fire damage, potable water, food or medicine poisoning or adulteration.[295]

§2. Environmental Criminal Law

452. The aforementioned hinders the development of the criminal aspect of environmental law and, what is more important, threatens the rule-unification of the criteria concerning sanctions. This means that at present, there exist several environmental causes in the different criminal courts of the country, but there are very few sentences.

I. Prosecution Agency for Research of Environmental Matters

453. This Prosecution Agency (whose acronym in Spanish is UFIMA) was established by Resolution 123, 2006 passed by the National Attorney General, within the legal frame of Article 120 of the National Constitution and Law 24946 from 1998 that is the organic law of the National Public Ministry which is made up of: (a) The Public Prosecution Ministry and General Prosecutors and, (b) The Public Ministry of Defence made up of the National General Defender and Public Defenders. This resolution implements a cooperation agreement between the National Attorney General and the SAyDS "in order to strengthen the eradication of crimes against the environment, whether they affect the environment in a direct or indirect way" as expressed in the first paragraph of Appendix I of said legal regulation.

Aiming to cover the whole Argentine territory, five "support points" are established "in order to act as link and cooperation in the coordination tasks" belonging

294. A person commits a damage crime who *'destroys, under-utilizes, makes disappear or in any way damages movable or immovable property, animal fully or partly alien to him when the crime does not constitutes another offense that could be severely punishable'* (Art. 183, Penal Code).

295. Article 186 of the Penal Code establishes: *'That a person who would cause fire, explosion or flooding, will be punished with three to ten years of imprisonment, if there was common damage to the goods'*. At the same time, Art. 200 establishes that *'Any individual who would poison, falsify or alter in any dangerous way to heath the potable water or food or medicine assigned to be used by people or collective use in a community, will be punished with three to ten years of imprisonment and a fine of ten thousands pesos'*.

to UFIMA with the corresponding general prosecutors being designated before the Courts of Appeals of all the country.

Some of the UFIMA missions are the followings: "to generate preliminary research" and "to support investigation underway" linked to environmental crimes, particularly those linked to Law 24051 of Hazardous Waste, crimes protecting public health and the environment (Articles 200–207 of the Criminal Code) and offences against Law 22241 on wild fauna protection and preservation, and other related crimes (Resolution National Attorney General 123/06 Article 3).

Out of 728 proceedings started by the UFIMA since its inception, 626 correspond to preliminary investigations and 102 to requests for cooperation.

§3. The Sanctions

454. The Argentine Criminal Code states prison or reclusion for most crimes expressed therein. Both sanctions are supposed to be accomplished 'by performing mandatory duties'[296] but reclusion is more severe than prison. We do not know the case of any person in Argentina who has been sent to jail for having committed an 'environmental crime'.

455. A 'damage' crime means 'destroying a movable, immovable thing or a totally or partially alien animal, rendering it useless or making it disappear or harm it in any way'. The penalty lasts from fifteen days to one year of prison and rises up to three months to four years provided that, in order to commit crime, 'poisonous or corrosive substances' are used'.[297]

456. 'To poison or adulterate potable water or food or medicinal substances for public use or consumption of a community in a dangerous way for health' is a crime sanctioned with three to ten years of prison (and a fine of up to ARS 200,000) which may rise from ten to twenty-five years if somebody dies as a consequence of it.[298] This also comprises the behaviour of a person who delivers, sells or distributes medicine or goods that are dangerous for health 'disguising its deleterious character'.[299]

457. The spreads of 'a dangerous and contagious disease' for 'people' is punished with reclusion or prison from three to fifteen years.[300]

296. Penal Code, Arts 6 and 9.
297. Articles 183 and 184 of the Penal Code.
298. Article 200 of the Penal Code.
299. Article 201*bis* of the Penal Code.
300. Article 202 of the Penal Code.

Part V. Juridical Actions of Individuals

Chapter 1. Administrative Remedies

§1. Definition and General Characteristics

458. Administrative remedies are legal actions brought by the holder of a subjective right or a legitimate interest against any act of the public administration, in order to request the public administration to comply with legal standards and regulations and, in fact, to modify or render the act ineffective and restore the aggrieved party's right or legitimate interest. Upon the filing of a remedy, the public administration may ratify, revoke or amend its act.[301]

459. The National Administrative Procedure Act 19549 of 1972 (LNPA) governs administrative acts and procedures. Administrative remedies are governed by Decree 1759 of 1972, which regulates the LNPA[302] except for the motion for review and the protection from administrative delay that are governed by the abovementioned law. The LNPA sets forth the basic administrative act and procedure requirements together with other provisions, are governed by its regulatory decree. Furthermore, according to this law, any officer who has been challenged or has refrained[303] from participating in the resolution of an administrative act shall not be entitled to take part in it.

301. For the differences between 'standing', 'subjective right', 'legitimate interest' and the recent developments in the concept of 'environmental standing' see Agustin Gordillo, *Tratado de Derecho Administrativo* (Buenos Aires: Fundación Derecho Administrativo, 2009), 2:1.
302. The National Administrative Procedure Act (LNPA in Spanish) and its regulatory decree are in force, as amended by Decree 1883 of 1991.
303. Article 6 of the LNPA of 1972 stresses: 'Officers and employees may be challenged under the provisions set forth in ss 17 and 18 of the National Civil and Commercial Procedure Code and notice thereof shall be served to their immediate superior within two days. The officer or employee's participation in the case should not constitute cause for challenging. If the challenged officer or employee admits the grounds and those grounds are admissible, the superior shall appoint an alternate officer or employee. Otherwise, the issue will be solved in five days. The term may be extended if evidence must be submitted. The challenging of officers and employees is governed by Art. 30 of the aforementioned Code and shall be immediately informed to their immediate superior, who should solve the problem within five days. If the challenge is accepted, an alternate officer or employee will be selected. Should the challenge be dismissed, the case will be remanded for further proceedings and the officer or employee will continue with the process. The resolutions issued as a result of the challenge or excuse and those deciding such issue shall not be appealed.'

460. In regard to the remedies' purpose, they shall only be brought against final administrative acts, that is, acts deciding on a particular issue. Therefore, no remedy can be brought against public administration's internal acts, such as the advisory bodies' opinions, orders and communications.[304]

461. It is worth analysing, from the practical point of view, whether the exhaustion of administrative remedies is mandatory to seek judicial action; strictly speaking, whether the exhaustion of administrative remedies is a condition for contesting administrative acts in Court. In Court, the procedure is called judicial review.

462. The administrative remedies are considered exhausted when the relevant minister performs the administrative action solving the issue. The SAyDS that functionally depends on the Cabinet is the current national environmental authority. Law 19549 of 1972 and its regulatory decree govern the administrative remedies and procedures before the national environmental authority.

463. In general, suing the national government requires the exhaustion of the administrative instance when trying to recover a payment made to government based on a settlement or the payment of an unduly paid tax or when a complaint for damages is filed against government based on any tort, unless otherwise stated in a provision.[305]

§2. The Remedies

464. Several administrative remedies can be brought against national administrative acts. They are the motion for administrative review and the appeal to a higher administrative authority. The remedy of complaint and the appeal from administrative delay must also be mentioned. Below, we will briefly explain each of them[306] to finish with the so-called complaint for illegitimacy formal remedy.

465. The motion for administrative review is governed by Articles 84–88 of Decree 1759 of 1972 and it is applicable against final acts or acts that completely prevent the aggrieved party from continuing with the claim. It is also applicable against procedural acts. It is filed with the administrative authority ordering the contested act to render it ineffective or amend it. There is ten-day term to file the remedy. Mentioned term starts running the following day the contested act was noticed. A practical aspect worth mentioning is that the motion for administrative review is not a mandatory condition for filing an appeal to a higher administrative authority.

304. Roberto Dromi, *Derecho Administrativo* (Ciudad Buenos Aires, Argentina, 1998), 930. Said author states that according to the aforementioned, the Office of the Treasury Attorney General has decided that no administrative remedy will be brought against procedural acts unless: they prevent the continuation of the administrative procedure (as in such case they are considered final acts) or damage a legitimate right or interest preventing the party from exercising its defence right.

305. These exceptions are set forth in Art. 32 of the LNPA of 1972.

306. Some provincial laws also govern the appeal, while national laws do not.

The law establishes that motions for administrative review inherently include appeals.

466. The appeal to a higher administrative authority is governed by Articles 89–93 of Decree 1759 of 1972. It can be directly brought, which means that there is no need to previously file a motion for administrative review. If the motion for administrative review was filed and dismissed, the appeal still remains in force as it is considered implicitly filed with the motion for administrative review. The appeal shall be directly filed within fifteen days as of notice of the contested act with the authority ordering such act and shall be submitted to the pertinent ministry within five days. Resolutions issued by the SAyDS are appealed before the Chief Cabinet Minister.

467. According to Article 22 of the LNPA, a motion for review can be filed when contradictions in the administrative act's provisions are found, when important documents of unknown existence are discovered after the performance of the administrative action, when such documents could not be submitted as evidence due to circumstances beyond control or are attributable to third-parties or upon violence, fraud or 'serious proven irregularity'.

468. According to Article 102 of Decree 1759 of 1972, a motion for clarification can be filed when the administrative act has contradictions between the cause of its performance and its provisions. It can be filed to correct mere material mistakes, to correct omissions or clarify aspects provided the substance of the act is not altered. The motion for clarification will be filed with the authority ordering the act within five days as of due notice.

469. An appeal can be brought against acts from decentralized agencies, autarchic entities or state-owned companies[307] and is governed by Articles 94–98 of Decree 1759 of 1972.

470. The remedy of complaint and the protection from administrative delay can be filed upon the public administration's inaction. They are considered two different remedies because the former is filed before the administrative authorities while the latter is filed in court. 'They can be *indistinctly* filed by the interested party and the filing of one of the remedies does not leave out the other.'[308] The remedy of complaint is governed by Articles 71 and 72 of Decree 1759 of 1972 and is filed with the immediate superior who ordered the act.

471. The protection from administrative delay is governed by Article 28 of the LNPA 19549 of 1972 and can be filed directly in court at any time.

---

307. It was also admitted against decisions made by a regulating agency in the case file *Aguas Argentinas SA v. Ente Tripartito de Obras y Servicios Sanitarios*, as Dr Roberto Dromi points out in his book *Administrative Law*, *supra*, 935.

308. R. Dromi, *supra*, 937.

472. Finally, a complaint for illegitimacy is a remedy made by an individual or legal entity who, having no personal and direct interest but having a simple interest files this remedy with the Public Administration to call the attention on an irregular act or fact. Dromi justifies this type of contest in the right to request to authorities, as stated in Article 14 of the NC, and also states that 'the complaint for illegitimacy shall be processed and decided by the Public Administration like any other remedy. Thus, the Executive Power or the Minister, as applicable, will issue a ruling based on the case'.[309]

309. R. Dromi, 942.

Chapter 2. Judicial Remedies

§1. Introduction

473. The legal system to contest administrative actions before judicial courts is governed by the LNPA 19549 of 1972. In other words, contesting an administrative act issued by a national authority such as the SAyDS, depends on whether it is a singular or general administrative act.

If the act is a singular administrative act such as, for example, a resolution denying the registration of a company under one of the hazardous waste register held by the SAyDS, it can be judicially contested[310] under four hypothesis: (1) if it is a final administrative act and the administrative remedies have been exhausted; (2) if the administrative act does not decide on the merits but completely prevents the processing of the claim imposed; (3) if there is administrative silence or ambiguity[311] and (4) if the administration violates any of its duties, according to Article 9 of the LNPA 19549 of 1972.[312]

474. However, in the case of a general administrative act being contested, such as, for example, a SAyDS' resolution on the new parameters to calculate the settlement and payment of an annual environmental fee, the administrative act can be contested[313] under two hypothesis: (1) if there is a prior administrative claim with an adverse result, or any of the provisions set forth in Article 10 occur, explain and (2) the authority proceeded with the act through final acts and the administrative remedies against those acts have been exhausted without positive results. Any claim against a national body government or any of its autarkic agencies shall be filed within ninety business days.

§2. General Rules on Judicial Jurisdiction

475. Regarding this subject it must be said that according to its structure as a federal state, the judicial jurisdiction in Argentina may be divided into two main categories: ordinary (provincial) and federal (national) jurisdiction.

310. Article 23 of LNPA.
311. The administrative silence vis-à-vis motions filed by individuals are negatively constructed, according to Art. 10 of LNPA, which states that 'the administrative silence or ambiguity vis-à-vis motions for a particular resolution shall be considered negative. Administrative silence can be considered positive only through express provisions. Should special provisions do not include a fixed term for the ruling, such ruling shall not exceed sixty days. Upon expiration of such term, the interested party shall request immediate release. If thirty days pass since the request of immediate release and no resolution is issued, then it should be considered that there is administrative silence'.
312. Article 9 of the LNPA requests the national administration to refrain from: (a) carrying out acts that may affect constitutional rights or guarantees; (b) acting while an administrative remedy is pending thus resulting in the suspension of its effects or having been solved, it is not notified.
313. Article 24, LNPA of 1972.

476. The legal rules applicable to judicial jurisdiction mainly spring up from proceeding norms and codes governing the different jurisdictions (civil and commercial, criminal and administrative). At the same time, many environmental norms usually called *'of content' or 'substantive'* by the doctrine – in opposition to other norms called *'procedural' or 'of form'*- contain precepts related to judicial competence. A clear example of this is Article 7 of the General Environment Law 25675 of 2002.[314]

477. With the intention of ordering this complex topic, we wish to emphasize that in Argentina the general rules on judicial jurisdiction are established in a general legal plexus and in particular environmental norms as well.

478. Among these general norms, we can find: (1) The NC which sets the jurisdiction: (i) originally from the CSJN (so-called original jurisdiction of Supreme Court of Justice, CSJN as per its acronym in Spanish) and (ii) the federal (or 'national') competence; (2) Law 48 of 1863; (3) the Decree-Law 1285 of 1958 which organizes the national justice; (4) the national Civil and Commercial Code relevant to civil procedures in which some environmental questions are shown; (5) the national Criminal Code for crimes with environmental consequences and; (6) the legal process relevant to administrative procedures in judicial seat.

479. As aforementioned, some environmental laws containing judicial competence-related norms have been enacted. Among them, we can mention: (1) the General Environmental Law 25675 of 2002, particularly Articles 7 and 32[315] and (2) the Hazardous Waste Law 24051 of 1992, Article 58.[316]

480. The environmental judicial competence is generally determined according to the specific characteristics of the case under trial: if it is dealing with environmental damages then the competence will be relevant to civil and commercial jurisdiction; if it is dealing with an environmental crime then it will be relevant to criminal jurisdiction and if the object of the case reflects upon the validity and lawfulness of an administrative case or state action or omission then it will be relevant to administrative procedure jurisdiction.

481. Due to hierarchy reasons, first, we will refer to original Supreme Court of Justice's jurisdiction regarding environmental matters and later on, the federal competence regarding the environment field that judges and federal courts have. Then

314. Some authors have pointed out that this law of minimum environmental standards also contains *'procedure environmental norms of minimum standards'* and because of their nature, they are applied throughout Argentine Republic, unlike common procedure norms that are applied in the provinces according to their respective proceedings codes.

315. This is because Art. 32 of this law does not contribute to figure out this important matter because it says: *'the environmental judicial competence will be the one subjected to ordinary norms of the competence'.*

316. Its Art. 58 establishes: *'The Federal Justice will be competent so as to know the criminal actions that will derive from this law.'*

we will analyse environmental competence in civil and commercial national processes and in national criminal causes due to crimes that affect the environment.

§3. Original Jurisdiction of the Supreme Court of Justice on Environmental Cases

482. In Argentina, the judicial cases can reach the CSJN through two ways. One way is through appeal. The other way has to do with the fact that the Court acts as Court of only decisive instance which means that the Supreme Court of Justice acts as the only instance. In this second case, it has *original* jurisdiction, that is, 'jurisdiction to consider a case in the first instance. Jurisdiction of court to take cognizance of a cause at its inception, try it and pass judgment upon the law and facts'.[317]

On 11 February 2014 the Office of Environmental Justice was set up by means of Executive Order 01/14 of the Supreme Court of Justice. This Office is dependent of the Supreme Court of Justice (CSJN) and is mainly in charge of: implementing and following up the actions derived from the Environmental Laws and the actions planned in the set-up of the Commission on Environmental Sustainability, both approved by Executive Orders of the Supreme Court of Justice issued in 2011 and 2013; developing relationships with similar national and international offices; coordinating training programs with the other branches and fostering the dissemination of decisions and initiatives related to the Environmental Justice at both national and international level. The Office of Environmental Justice involves three areas devoted to training, data collection and research.

483. Also, original jurisdiction of the Supreme Court of Justice (CSJN) may exist under two hypotheses: when a province is part in a lawsuit, and when ambassadors, ministers and foreign consuls are involved.[318] At the same time, and as Esaín[319] points out, that original jurisdiction *'in the cases when a province is sued [original jurisdiction] can be extended in favour of, not only the province judges according to Article 12.4 law 48 but also the lower federal courts, mainly since the doctrine of the Flores case'.*

317. This is how 'original jurisdiction' is defined by the Black's Law Dictionary. *Black's Law Dictionary with Pronunciations*, 6th edn (Minnesota: West Publishing Co, 1990), 1099.
318. Articles 116 and 117 of the NC state that the knowledge and decision of every cause that deals with the items by the Constitution and by the laws of the nation correspond to the Supreme Court and to the lower court in s. 12 of Art. 75; and by the treaties with foreign nations; of the cases regarding ambassadors, ministers and foreign consuls; of admiralty and maritime jurisdiction cases; of such cases where the Nation takes part; of those cases between two provinces; between the neighbours of one province and the neighbours of another province; between the neighbours of different provinces; within a province or between its neighbours, against a state or foreign citizen. Article 117 reads: In these cases the Supreme Court will exercise its jurisdiction by appeal according to rules and exceptions that the Congress prescribes; but in such cases where it deals with ambassadors, ministers and foreign consuls and in which a province is involved, then the Supreme Court will exclusively exercise it.
319. José Alberto Esaín, *supra*, 857.

§4. Federal Jurisdiction on Environmental Conflicts

484. According to Esaín, whose work we consider complete and updated, judicial competence in the environmental arena is – by rule- local (provincial level) and only in certain exceptional cases it corresponds to federal justice (national level). Due to this fact, the provincial competence is defined by exclusion: the awareness and decision of every cause that is not relevant to a federal jurisdiction will then be relevant to the provincial jurisdiction.

485. The doctrine is testimony that the federal jurisdiction is established according the following criteria: *ratione personae*, *ratione materiae* and *ratione loci.*

486. In environmental causes, the federal jurisdiction *ratione personae* proceeds when the Nation, or when any national autarkic entity takes part in a trial. Refer to the procedural concept of *party* implies that plaintiff, defendant, third party or co-defendant are understood to be included in it.[320] At the same time, this extends to the cases when suits are filed against the national environmental authority (SAyDS) because of control faults or omissions under its responsibility.

487. The environmental federal jurisdiction *ratione materiae* fundamentally corresponds to those conflicts affecting inter-jurisdictional natural resources. According to the legal principles that are the essence of every federal state and that follow uniformly jurisprudence precedents, the general environmental Law 25675 of 2002 establishes the federal jurisdiction *ratione materiae* in Article 7, whose second paragraph establishes that '[i]n those cases where the act, omission or generated situation effectively leads to, degradation, pollution of inter-jurisdictional environmental resources, the competence will then be federal.'

488. The doctrine[321] considers that in order to determine whether inter-jurisdictional environmental systems have been altered, then the following should be first proved: (a) if there ever existed contamination and if this was so, potential contamination is not included. However, a possible contamination in the future can be taken into account, if certain to occur; (b) which is the geographic area affected and (c) if it exceeds any local border.

489. The CSJN substantially changed its doctrine since Article 7 of the LGA was in force. As Esaín sharply analyses, such evolution can be seen in its judgments *'Roca Magdalena'*[322] passed when Article 41 of the NC was in force according to

320. This covers the Coast Guard, National Park Administration, The National Commission on Atomic Power and the Nuclear Regulatory Authority when it is about entities that have a huge number of environmental competencies. Esaín, *supra*, 720.

321. Esaín stresses that the National Supreme Court of Justice currently has a criterion according to which in case of environmental damage with possible inter-jurisdictional effects the competence corresponds to federal judges in accordance with the second paragraph Art. 7 of the General Environmental Law 25675 of 2002. Said author points out that this criterion of the Court matches with that of the majority of lower court judgments. *Supra*, 51, 775.

322. In which it was determined in favour of the provincial competence in environmental damage.

1994 reform, and *'Fundación Medam'*[323] passed on 9 September 2004 that is, after Law 25675 of 2002, Article 7 was in force.

490. Unlike what happens with *ratione personae*, the competence *ratione materiae* cannot be extended.

Next Page is Argentina – 149

323. In this case, however, the Court determined the conflict in favour of the federal jurisdiction.

491. The federal jurisdiction *ratione loci* is in force since the 1994 constitutional reform only takes place in the national utility institutions'[324] where environmental conflicts can be presented.[325] In these suppositions the so-called *doctrine of non-interference-* applies, which implies that only the federal competence is necessary to achieve the purposes of such institution.

§5. The Procedure before the Civil Court

492. The national Commercial and Civil Procedures Code sets a general rule vis-à-vis competence: this is determined by the nature of the plaintiff's claims and not from the defences or exceptions made by the defendant.[326] This is a general rule about judicial jurisdiction.

493. According to what an Argentine scholar in Law of Civil Procedure teaches: 'in order to decide which the competent judge is, there is no point in conforming to the law which in fact can be applicable, but to the one regarded as foundation of the filed lawsuit'.[327]

I. The Competent Court

494. In Argentina, the jurisdiction of the civil courts may be determined by the place where environmental damage appears, or by its nature. If the civil liability is claimed on the basis of a contract the competent judge will be that of the place where it was signed or where it has effects according to the cases. If the civil action is founded on extra-contractual liability, the competent judge will be that of the place where liability was generated or in the place of the defendant's address.

495. The legal doctrine highlights that:

> provisional measures can be pronounced with full efficacy even in the case of incompetence, and they remain even when this competence does not apply.

---

324. Such are the places where there is the pursuance of certain goals that are in the Nation's general interests. Regarding this, the NC establishes that is in the Congress's accountability: *'[t]o exercise an exclusive legislation on the territory of the capital and pass the necessary legislation for the end purposes enforcement of the national utility entities in the Republic territory. Provincial and municipal authorities keep policing powers and its obligation over these entities, while they do not interfere with such purposes' enforcement'* (Art. 75 subs. 30).

325. Before the 1994 reform to the national Constitution federal jurisdiction existed also on the so-called *national territories*. But this supposition lacks validity today. It was linked to historical reasons, when Argentina was not politically integrated and there still existed these kinds of territories.

326. Article 5 of the national Civil Procedure and Commercial Code, that identically correlates to Article No. 5 of the Provincial Civil Procedure and Commercial Code of Buenos Aires.

327. Augusto Mario Morello, *Códigos Procesales en lo Civil y Comercial de la Provincia de Buenos Aires y de la Nación. Comentados y Anotados*, 2nd edn (Buenos Aires: Editorial Platense – Abeledo Perrot, 2003), II A:71,154. Professor Morello cites there the doctrine concurrent with the National Supreme Court of Justice published in Fallos 279:95 and 286:45.

> They cannot be reversed under any argument saying that the judge who dictated them was incompetent because, even thought that may be true, the constitutional imperative of preventing deleterious activities of the environment health, current population and future generations determines the maintenance of these remedies because the strength and efficacy of the preventive mandate reaches this point, if necessary.[328]

496. The procedure before a province's civil court is ruled by each provincial Civil and Commercial Procedures Code.[329] These codes follow, in general, the principles established by the national Civil and Commercial Code of Procedures. Some differences must be noted: many Argentine provinces have organized the so-called Justice of Peace system enabled to decide cases where minimum monetary cases are involved. That was also, in the past, the case in the city of Buenos Aires.[330]

497. In the city of Buenos Aires, as it is the capital of the country, the national (federal) Civil and Commercial Procedures Code is applicable to procedures before the national Civil Judges of First Instance and also to procedures before the national Commercial Judges of First Instance (and the corresponding national Civil and Commercial Courts of Appeals).

498. In the city of Buenos Aires, there also exist judicial Courts with exclusively local jurisdiction. Such jurisdiction does not belong either to the national or to the provincial area. Specifically, in the CABA, there exists a Supreme Court of Justice that functions according to its own Code of Administrative Procedures.[331] Such court has jurisdiction to intervene in local environmental matters.

§6. The Criminal Courts

I. The Criminal Procedure Code

499. The rules of the criminal procedure are contained in the Criminal Procedure Code adopted by Law 23984 of 1991 whose Book I establishes the following basic principles of the occidental criminal law: nobody can be judged by any other judge rather than the appointed one in accordance with the Constitution and competent ones according to their regulatory laws, nor even punished without previous

328. Héctor Jorge Bibiloni, *El proceso Ambiental* (Buenos Aires: Lexis Nexis Argentina, 2005), 216–217. As a back-up to the thesis, the author cites the doctrine of the case *Sagarduy Alberto v. Copetro SA* et al. published in LLBA 1995-937 with comments by Carlos A. Botassi.
329. In the province of Buenos Aires, for example, the provincial Civil and Commercial Judges of First Instance have competence on both civil and commercial issues. The National Civil Judges of First Instance in the city of Buenos Aires have only competence on civil matters, apart from that of the National Commercial Judges of First Instance.
330. Similarly to the Peace Judges in the province of Buenos Aires, the city of Buenos Aires had the National Special Judges for the Federal Capital of Buenos Aires, who existed until they were converted into National Civil Judges of First Instance.
331. Said Procedure Code complements the law of administrative processes of the city of Buenos Aires, and was adopted due to the law of the city of Buenos Aires 189 passed on 22 Jun. 1999.

trial grounded on laws enacted before the fact in question and substantiated in accordance with said Code. Nobody can be considered guilty of a crime until there is a firm sentence declaring so. No one can be legally judged two times based on the same event. This jurisdiction cannot be extended. The analogical interpretation is forbidden and in case of doubt, the judge must consider 'what is most favourable to the accused'.[332]

500. If a person is accused of committing a national and federal jurisdictional crime, he must be judged first, by the federal jurisdiction. This does not prevent the simultaneous proceeding of one trial with another one, provided the procedure in the national jurisdiction does not interfere with the federal one.[333]

501. The Criminal Procedure Code allows two civil actions to be carried out (for monetary compensation) before criminal judges, but the regulation establishes that it is known as 'the criminal and civil cases interdependence' according to which, the civil sentence (punishes to pay for damage and loss) cannot be pronounced unless there exists criminal sentence. Still, a criminal judge can absolve the accused of a crime and sentence him in the civil field. However, in the professional practice, civil actions are not exercised before criminal judges but before civil judges.[334]

502. The CSJN rules according to its jurisdiction stated by the NC The national Chamber of Cassation of Criminal Matters of the Capital Federal rules unconstitutional, cassation and review appeals. The national Chamber of Appeals rules the appeals against the decisions of the examining magistrates, among others.

503. In general terms, the competencies of the first instance criminal judges[335] are divided into the competencies corresponding to the examining magistrates and the judges in correctional matters. The examining magistrates have competence to deal with public action crimes, while judges in correctional matters have competence to deal with crimes sanctioned with penalties that are non-depriving of liberty and depriving of liberty up until three years.[336]

504. The Criminal Procedure Code also sets the rules for the competence of the Federal Court in Criminal matters and that of the federal judge.[337]

505. As a subsidiary rule, Article 38 of the national Criminal Procedure Code establishes that if the circumstances that surrounded the crime are doubted or ignored, then the competent judge will be the one who started the legal proceedings.

332. Articles 1–3 and 18, Criminal Procedure Code.
333. Article 20, Criminal Procedure Code.
334. Article 16, Criminal Procedure Code.
335. We mention this because juvenile courts and judges also exist (Arts 28 y 29 of the Criminal Procedure Code states their competencies) and also the criminal enforcement judges (Book V of the Criminal Procedure Code states their competencies).
336. Articles 26–27, Criminal Procedure Code.
337. Articles 32–33, Criminal Procedure Code.

II. Specific Criminal Regulations: Hazardous Waste

506. However, and specifically in the hazardous waste arena, Chapter IX of the national Hazardous Waste Law 24051 of 1992 has a particular crime regime. In this chapter, not only federal competence to judge crimes categorized by such regulations but also criminal offences in Articles 55, 56 and 57 are established.

507. The sanctioned behaviours by Article 55 are: the use of waste to poison, adulterate or contaminate soil, water, atmosphere or the environment in general in a dangerous way for health. The punishment for this crime is three to ten years of prison and a fine of 10,000 to 200,000 pesos. If the action were followed by death, the punishment comprises ten to twenty-five years of confinement or prison.

508. If any of these crimes considered by Article 55 of the Hazardous Waste Law was committed by recklessness or negligence or lack of skill in its own profession or non-observance of regulations, then Article 56 states that the punishment lasts from a month to two years of prison. If there is sickness or death of a person, then such punishment is from six months to three years.

509. Furthermore, Article 57 is related to those who manage or administer legal entities. It is applied when any of the crimes in Article 55 or 56 were committed by the decision of a legal entity. In such suppositions, the punishment will be imposed on directors, managers, union members, security board members and administrators, apart from the other criminal responsibilities that may have existed.

III. The Competent Court

510. Article 37 of the national Criminal Procedure Code establishes, as a general rule, that a competent judge is the criminal judge with jurisdiction on the place where the crime was committed. If it is about a permanent or continuing offence the competent judge will be that of the place where the offence finished.

511. In case of attempted crime, that is, if a person starts to commit it but does not finishes it due to reasons not pertaining to him, then the competent judge is the one with jurisdiction over the place where the last action was committed.

§7. The Environmental Statutory Protection Action

512. Statutory Protection originates in habeas corpus -created in the *Magna Carta* signed by King John I of England in 1215 – to protect individual liberty and free movement of people who were illegally bereft of their freedom.

Argentina followed that trend and since the beginning of the Republic stepped into to obtain a judgment to rapidly protect those who underwent an open violation of their rights protected by the NC as a solution to the absence of any other suitable way of proceeding to redress such grievances.

513. Thus, the statutory protection was a product of jurisprudence creation of the CSJN fundamentally through its judgments on the cases *Siri* (statutory protection brought against public authority action) and *Kot* (in which the Supreme Court expanded the application scope sustaining its origin against individual actions).[338]

With the passing of law 16986 of 1966 the necessary requisite to admit a statutory protection is the inexistence of procedure, judicial or administrative redress which allows obtaining the protection of the violated right (Article 2, subsection a).

514. The *environmental* statutory protection did not exist in the Argentine legislation until the 1994 constitutional reform. The environmental statutory protection is expressly regulated under Article 43 of the NC, a regulation that is complemented with Article 30 of Law 25675 of 2002.

515. According to Article 43 of the NC, any person may file a prompt and summary action of 'statutory protection' whenever no other legal remedy exists, against any act or omission by public authorities or by private individuals, that presently or imminently harms, restricts, alters or threatens, in an arbitrary or manifestly illegal manner, the rights and guarantees recognized by the NC, by a treaty, or by a law. As appropriate, the judge may declare the norm upon which the harmful act or omission is founded unconstitutional. When this action regards any form of discrimination, or the rights that protect the environment, competition, the user, the consumer, or rights of a collective nature in general, it may be brought by the affected party, the ombudsman and the associations that support these ends that are registered as required by a law that shall determine the requirements and forms of their organization.

516. The party concerned, the ombudsman and NGO's with environmental purposes are recognized as entitled with legal standing to present environmental statutory protection.

The figure of the *party concerned* as a person with standing to file this action has two environmental cases as precedents, which had a great impact on mass media.[339]

517. We share the doctrine opinion, which states that in order for the statutory protection to be in force, it is no requisite for the absence or exhaustion, if any at any time, of any administrative channels exist.

518. As Gelli rightly considers: '[j]udges posses a great deal of space to measure, in concrete cases and in every defendant specific situation, not the existence of another oral legal channel but the minor suitability of the legal remedy seen in the legal order to protect the violated right'.[340] And he keeps on remembering that

---

338. Caso *Siri Angel s/ Interpone recurso de Habeas Corpus*, CSJN, Fallos 239:459 (1957). Caso *Kot, Samuel SRL s/ Recurso de Habeas Corpus*, CSJN Fallos 241:291 (1958).

339. According to María Angélica Gelli, *supra*, v. 1, 622 such cases are *Kattan, Alberto and others v. Poder Ejecutivo Nacional* published in ED, 105–245 related to a statutory protection against the fishing of dolphins authorized by the national government and *Ekmekdjian v. Sofovich* published in CSJN Fallos 315:1492.

340. María Angélica Gelli, *supra*, v. 1, 613.

in the case of *'Comunidad Indígena del Pueblo Wichi Hoktek T'Oi'* the National Supreme Court of Justice made proper use of the statutory protection argument about the existence and possible aggravation of the environmental damages that the elimination of the forest would produce – climatic changes, biodiversity alterations and desertification- and the individual aggravations of all the Community members that may also be produced, and understood that the court from Salta did not sufficiently sustain the argument for those situations'.[341]

519. A more recent environmental statutory protection case involved interpretation of the minimum environmental standards for the protection of the glaciers and periglacial regions.[342]

Another important case was decided in 2009 by the Federal Chamber of Appeals of Mar del Plata regarding the uncontrolled fishing of the merluza *hubssi* and the legal protection of the rights of collective incidence as recognized by the General Law of the Environment 25675 of 2002.[343]

341. *Ibid.*
342. *Asociación Civil Diálogo por el Ambiente v. PEN s/ Amparo Ambiental*, published by the environmental suplement of www.eldial.com.ar of 20 Apr. 2010 (accessed 29 Jun. 2011).
343. *Cámara Pesquera Marplatense v. Estado Nacional s/ Acción de Amparo*, published by www.eldial.com.ar www.eldial.com/nuevo/archivo-jurisprudencia-detalle.asp?base=14&t=j&id=23894&id_publicar=19259&fecha_publicar=11/12/2009&numero_edicion=2922&titulo_rojo=Jurisprudencia%20Federal&numingr=4&usr=13890292 (accessed 12 Feb. 2011).

Selected Bibliography

Aldaya M.M., et al. 'Strategic Importance of Green Water in International Crop Trade'. In *Value of Water Research Series Nº 25*, UNESCO-IHE Institute for Water Education, Delft, the Netherlands in collaboration with University of Twente, Enschede, the Netherlands and Delft University of Technology, Delft, the Netherlands. March 2008. www.unesco-ihe.org/ ... /Report25GreenWater InternationalTrade.pdf. 18 September 2000.

Bibiloni Héctor, J. *El Proceso Ambiental*. Buenos Aires: Lexis Nexis Argentina, 2005.

Bloch Roberto. 'El Valor del Agua Dulce en la Supervivencia de la Humanidad'. In *Agenda Internacional Nº 5*.

Boyle Alan, E. 'Marine Pollution under the Law of the Sea Convention'. In *Law of the Sea,* edited by HE Judge Hugo Caminos. England: Ashgate Dartmouth – The Library of Essays in International Law, 2001.

Caron David. *Analyzing and Understanding Treaties in the Area of International Environmental Law*. American University Washington School of Law. Sine data. www.wcl.american.edu/environment/iel/caron.cfm.

Caminos Hugo. *Law of the Sea*. England, Ashgate Dartmouth, The Library of Essays in International Law, 2001, Book review by Dr Julio César Villano. Accessible on: www.estudiovillano.com/estudio-villano-abogados-recursos-publicaciones-articulos.html.

Cantano Alis. *El Convenio Marpol 73/78 – Un Estudio Detallado*. Ministerio de Medioambiente del Reino Unido. Accessible on the internet: www.derecho maritimo.info/pagina/marpol.htm#II.-%20PROTECCI%C3%93N%20JUR%C3% 8DDICA%20DEL%20MEDIO%20MARINO.

Canter Larry, W. *Manual de Evaluación de Impacto Ambiental: Técnicas para la Elaboración de los Estudios de Impacto*. Madrid: McGraw-Hill Interamericana de España S.A.U., 1998. Segunda Edición.

Esaín José Alberto. *Competencias Ambientales*. Buenos Aires: Abeledo Perrot, 2008.

Ferrey Steven. *Environmental Law*. 4th edn. New York: Aspen Publishers Wolters Kluwer Law & Business, 2007.

Grassetti Eduardo, R. *Estudios Ambientales*. Buenos Aires: Editorial Heliasta, 1998.

Iribarren Federico Jesús. *Evaluación de Impacto Ambiental: su Enfoque Jurídico*. Buenos Aires: Ediciones Universo, 1997.

Lorente Aznar César, J. *Empresa, Derecho y Medio Ambiente*. Barcelona: J.M. Bosch Editor S.A., 1996.

Selected Bibliography

Kirchner Andree (ed). *International Marine Environmental Law. Institutions, Implementation and Innovations*. The Netherlands: Kluwer Law International – International Environmental Law & Policy Series, 2003.

Maes Frank (ed). *Marine Resource Damage Assessment: Liability and Compensation for Environmental Damage*. The Netherlands: Springer, 2005.

Malone Linda, A. *Environmental Law*. New York: Emanuel® Law Outlines – Aspen Publishers Wolters Kluwer Law & Business, 2007.

Mosset Iturraspe Jorge, et al. *Daño Ambiental*. Buenos Aires: Rubinzal Culzoni, 1999.

Percival Robert V., et al. *Environmental Regulation: Law, Science and Policy*. 5th edn. New York: Aspen Publishers a Wolters Kluwer Business, 2006.

Pigretti Eduardo, A. *Derecho Ambiental Profundizado*. Buenos Aires: La Ley, 2004.

Shelton Dinah & Kiss Alexandre. *Judicial Handbook on Environmental Law*. United Nations Environmental Program (UNEP), United Kingdom, 2005.

Valls Mario, F. *Manual de Derecho Ambiental*. Buenos Aires: Abeledo Perrot, 2008.

Valls Mariana. *Derecho Ambiental*. Buenos Aires: Ciudad Argentina, 1999.

Villano Julio César. 'Contaminación de aguas: Reseña al fallo'. (Corte d' Appello di Milano. La Giustizia Penale, Roma, año XCVI, núm II, febrero 1991, parte segunda, p. 119). (La Ley, Buenos Aires, 1993) tomo A, 1215–1216. Quoted in Global Judges Symposiom on Sustainable Development and the Role of Law: The Argentine Case. (Johannesburg, South Africa, 18–20 August 2002), 53. Accesible through the internet on: www.unep.org/law/Symposium/Judges_symposium.htm.

Villano Julio César. *Principal Environmental Law Treaties and Argentine Law: Particular Reference to the International Ship and Port Facility Code (ISPS Code)*. Indian Society of International Law (ISIL). Paper presented to the '5th International Law Conference' Nueva Delhi, India. 8–9 December 2007.

Wooley David QC, et al. *Environmental Law*. 2nd edn. London: Oxford University Press, 2009.

Zlata Drnas de Clément. *The Environmental Precautionary Principle with Particular Reference to the Law of the Sea*. Annals of Maritime Studies 2003. On internet: Academia Nacional de Derecho y Ciencias Sociales de Córdoba: www.acader.unc.edu.ar.

Zhu Ling. *Compulsory Insurance and Compensation for Bunker Oil Pollution Damage*. International Max Planck Research School for Maritime Affairs at the University of Hamburg. Hamburg Studies on Maritime Affairs. Vol 5. Berlin Heidelberg: Springer-Verlag, 2007.

Official Documents

Primer Informe Estado del Ambiente 2010, Secretaría de Ambiente y Desarrollo Sustentable de la Nación (SAyDS). En internet se encuentra disponible el índice, en la siguiente dirección: www.ambiente.gov.ar/aplicaciones/home/menu_novedades/files/informe_ambiente.pdf.

Annual Environmental Law Report, Fundación Ambiente y Recursos Naturales (FARN) 2009. On the internet it is available through the following electronic address: http://farn.org.ar/docs/FARN%20Annual%20Environmental%20Report %202009- %20English%20Version.pdf.

International Oil Pollution Claims Manual 2008, IOPC Fund 1992. www.iopcfund.org/npdf/2008%20claims%20manual_e.pdf.

Encyclopaedia

Enciclopedia Jurídica 1ra Edición. Wolters Kluwer España. Enrique Arnaldo Alcubilla (General Coordinator). Madrid, Wolters Kluwer España SA, 2008–2009. (The twenty-three volumes of this masterpiece refer to Spanish law and contain clear concepts and explanations which are applicable to countries having their legal system based on continental and civil law principles. In particular, see the voice *Medio Ambiente* in v. 14, pps. 7899–7904).

Selected Bibliography

Index

The numbers here refer to paragraph numbers.

Index

Index

www.ingramcontent.com/pod-product-compliance
Lightning Source LLC
Chambersburg PA
CBHW071343230926
51846CB00002B/430
9789041161628